A GREAT WEEKEND IN

BARCELONA

A GREAT WEEKEND IN BARCELONA

The spellbinding Catalan capital

Barcelona is a city of contrasts set between the mountains and the sea, a tireless reveller by night and hard-working by day, fervently European yet fiercely Catalan. *Seny* – common sense – and *rauxa* – a touch of madness – make it fluctuate between tradition and innovation. Loyal to its past, but ever reaching out towards new galaxies, it combines imagination with a sharp nose for business.

'It isn't possible to talk of one Barcelona, because Barcelona is made up of several distinct interwoven elements. Archaeologists ought to know why eternal cities are made up of archaeological layers, as if the place they chose for their existence was the result of a vague yet inevitable plan,' observed Manuel Vázquez Montalbán in his *Barcelonas*. Notable travellers of the 1930s, such as Joseph Kessel, and those associated with the Civil War, like George Orwell and Ernest Hemingway,

wouldn't recognise the port areas of the city today. The slogan of the 1990s, 'Make Barcelona Beautiful' inspired architectural projects galore, which have transformed this former legendary stronghold of resistance to Francoism. With the arrival of the Olympic Games in 1992, Barcelona decided to buck up its ideas and with envigorating enthusiasm several of its old quarters have been given a creative and well thought-out face-lift.

The capital of Catalonia burst into frenzied action and museums, shops, restaurants, bars and galleries flourished. Modernity, creativity and the Catalan identity blended to produce a visual feast. From old-fashioned town houses to the latest bars and from the traditional charm of a cabaret in the Barrio Chino to the stunts of an acrobat on the Ramblas, you'll find yourself in the middle of a forward-looking city, full of life and colour, but also proud of its past. Indeed, the people of Barcelona take their roots very seriously. Holidays and festivals follow on one from another in a whirlwind of tradition. Southern European

in terms of their fierce pride and attachment to tradition, northern European in terms of their work ethic and business acumen, Catalans cultivate their identity as others cultivate their prize blooms – jealously and with care.

Wander through the labyrinth of narrow streets and you may come across a delightful shaded patio concealing a collection of Picassos, or sit on the terrace of the Plaça del Pi and sip a *horchata*

to the sound of an amateur saxophone player. If you like to sample the food of a city as well as its atmosphere, try La Boqueria, the covered market situated on the Ramblas, which is a riot of colour and delicious smells, and everything that a mediterranean market should be. Try some dried fruit and nuts for a snack and then head for the port and the revitalised shoreline of Barceloneta. Lined with trendy

restaurants and designer bars you can sample *copas* and *tapas* and watch families out for their Sunday afternoon consitutionals. It's a city that rarely sleeps. Catalans say with a superior air, that siestas are for Andalusians. Barcelona nights are neon-lit, retro, rococo, sequined or high-tech. Adopt the Catalan mentality of work hard and play hard, and embark on a round of the bars. You'll need a lot of stamina and the ability to stay awake well into the small hours. The people of Barcelona certainly know how to enjoy life. However, whether you're a party animal or more inclined to stroll around admiring the architecture, you'll just love your weekend in Barcelona.

How to get there

The ideal seasons for visiting Barcelona are the spring and autumn. From March onwards, you'll start to encounter the heat, but be on the lookout for frequent showers around Easter. Several big religious festivals light up the streets between March and June.

HOW TO GET THERE

For a great weekend in Barcelona, the best way to get there is probably by plane. From the UK and Ireland, the flight takes approximately two and a half hours. From the USA, Canada and Australasia, it is, of course, considerably longer and invariably requires a stopover, though there are some direct flights (see details below). From continental Europe, the train is also an option, though probably only if you're going for more than a couple of days, since it may require a night on board. The train journey from the UK can take up to 30 hours (see p. 6).

When to go

Temperatures can soar to as high as 37°C/99°F in July and August, so avoid the summer months if you can't stand the heat and crowds of tourists. However, cultural activity is at its height in July, with the Greek theatre staging musical entertainment and plays and bringing together foreign and Catalan companies. From 15 August for two weeks, Barcelona is the centre for the unique traditional celebrations of Gràcia (see p. 16). September and October remain sunny and the Diada, the national holiday on 11 September, is very enjoyable. If you do decide to go at the end of autumn or in winter, don't worry about the cold as the climate is still mild at that time of year, though temperatures can fall to below 7°C/45°F at night in February. You could also join in the celebrations at Christmas and New Year (see p. 14). On 5th/6th January the Festa del Reis takes place – the Festival of the Three Kings, or the Three Wise Men, when children traditionally receive their presents.

FLIGHTS FROM THE UK

British Airways
www.british-airways.com
☎ 08457 77 333 77
Regular flights to Barcelona – call for schedules.

Virgin Express
☎ 020 7744 0004
www.virgin-express.com
Has flights from Heathrow, Stansted and Gatwick – all of which go via Brussels.

Iberia
☎ 0845 601 2854
www.iberia.com
Has 3 flights a day from Heathrow to Barcelona and one per day from Manchester.

Easyjet
☎ 0870 6000 000
www.easyjet.com
Offer cheaper 'no-frills' flights to Barcelona. Book as far as possible in advance for the bargain fares.

Go
☎ 0870 607 6543
www.go-fly.com
Another low cost airline which flies out of Stansted. Book well in advance for the best deals.

FROM IRELAND

British Airways
☎ (00 44) 191 490 7901
www.british-airways.com
Offer flights from Shannon, Cork, and Dublin to Barcelona via London Gatwick.

Iberia
☎ 01-407-3017
www.iberia.com
Offer one direct flight per day from Dublin to Barcelona. Flights from other cities in Ireland go via Dublin.

FROM THE USA AND CANADA

British Airways
☎ 1-800-AIRWAYS
www.british-airways.com
Daily flights via London from all over the USA and Canada.

Delta
☎ 1-800-241-241
www.delta-air.com
Has some direct flights to Barcelona via JFK. Call for more information.

TAKING CARE OF YOUR BUDGET

Barcelona is no longer a particularly cheap destination. Spain, like Italy and Greece, is nowadays as expensive as any other European country. Hotel prices have also risen quite considerably in recent years and of course prices in the city inevitably tend to be higher than in the smaller towns.

For two people, you should consider budgeting for around €150-200 a day for good accommodation, meals and outings.And if you really want the best deal available, make sure you ask for the 'fin de semana' price (see p. 71), when you book your hotel room.

You can expect to pay €18-35 for a meal, from €5-6 for a museum ticket, €0.85 for a bus ticket, €1.80-3.60 for a non-alcoholic drink, €6-12 for a disco, €15 for a concert seat, and up to €1.10 to send a postcard to Australia.

Iberia
☎ 1-800-772-4642
www.iberia.com
Offer direct flights – call for more information.

FROM AUSTRALIA AND NEW ZEALAND
There are no direct flights to Barcelona from Australia and New Zealand, but it's possible to stop over in other European cities, such as London, en route. Check with your travel agent for flight details or try looking on the web.

BY TRAIN
Most international trains arrive in Barcelona at the Estació de França (metro Barceloneta). If you're arriving in Barcelona from within Spain, you'll arrive at Estació Sants (metro Sants Estació). It's a long journey from the UK or Ireland and you'll need to allow between 20 and 30 hours! If you do decide to take the train, your trip will, of course, include crossing the English Channel,

which you can do by ferry or by taking the Eurostar (☎ 08705 186 186 www.eurostar.com) to Paris. From there you could take the Trenhotel ('hotel train'), an overnight service offering sleeper accommodation. The journey takes just over 12 hours and you should ask at one of the rail companies listed about this service.

European Rail
☎ 020 7387 0444 (UK)
www.europeanrail.co.uk

Rail Europe
10 Leake Street
London SE1 7NN
☎ 0870 584 8848 (UK)

Or ask your travel agent for more information. If you need information about rail services within Spain, call the national rail operator RENFE on ☎ 93 490 02 02 (domestic), or ☎ 93 490 11 22 (international).

BY COACH
The journey by coach can take up to a whole day, so it isn't really an option for just a weekend. However, you

GETTING USED TO THE EURO
From the 1 January 2002 the euro will replace the official currency of 12 European nations, including Spain. The peseta will cease to be legal tender on 28 February 2002, although banks will still exchange notes and coins after this date. The euro, which is divided into 100 cents, has a fixed exchange rate of 166.386 pesetas. There are plenty of cash machines in the city and you can withdraw cash easily using a credit card. If you need to carry large sums of money around with you, it's better to take traveller's cheques as pick-pocketing is rife in the city.

might consider taking a coach if you're going for a slightly longer break. From the UK there are regular bus services to Spain. Eurolines (☎ 08705 143 219) has services to Barcelona. Ask at major travel agencies, or visit their website at www.eurolines.co.uk for more information. Within Barcelona, buses usually arrive at Estació del Nord (metro Arc de Triomf), though some international buses arrive at Estació de Sants.

Estació del Nord
☎ 93 265 65 08.

Estació de Sants
☎ 93 490 40 00.

FROM THE AIRPORT TO THE CITY CENTRE

The airport of Prat, 12km/7 miles south of Barcelona, is linked to the city by way of the Castelldefels motorway. There are various ways for you to get to the centre.

BY TRAIN

From 6am to 10pm, it takes 25 minutes to get to the Sants and Plaça de Catalunya station, with departures every half-hour. Tickets cost 350 ptas/€2.10.

BY AIRPORT BUS

From 6.30am to 11pm, a bus leaves every quarter of an hour for the Plaça de Catalunya, stopping at the Plaça d'Espanya and Plaça de la Universitat. Tickets cost 475 ptas/€2.85 and the journey takes half an hour.

BY TAXI

For a cost of 2,500 ptas/€15, you can reach the city centre in half an hour.

Airport information
☎ 93 298 38 38.

Transport information
☎ 93 412 00 00.

CUSTOMS

In June 1999 duty-free allowances were abolished between EU countries,

therefore EU citizens can take up to 800 cigarettes, 90 litres of wine and 10 litres of spirits when leaving Spain. If you enter Spain from a non-EU country, however, you can only take with you 200 cigarettes, 2 litres of wine, 1 litre of spirits and 60cl of perfume duty-free.

FORMALITIES

EU-citizens only require an identity card or passport. Citizens of the USA, Canada, Australia and New Zealand don't require a visa, just a passport. Foreign embassies are all located in Madrid.

UK
☎ 91 319 02 00
Calle de Fernando el Santo
USA
☎ 91 587 22 00
Calle de Serrano, 75

Canada
☎ 91 431 43 00
Calle de Nuñde Balboa, 35

Australia
☎ 91 431 43 00
Plaza del Descubridor
Diego de Ordás 3-2,
Edificio Santa Engracia, 120

New Zealand
☎ 91 523 02 26
Plaza de la Lealtad, 2

HEALTH AND INSURANCE

No vaccinations are needed for travel in Spain. EU citizens

LOCAL TIME

Spain is one hour ahead of GMT, except from the end of March to the end of September, when the difference is 2 hours. To sample the true Catalan lifestyle, you really need to adjust to the times of meals. Lunch is usually between 1.30pm and 2pm, and dinner is eaten very late, at 10pm. Shops are generally shut between 2pm and 4pm (see p. 84), and banks and museums are generally open all day (until 7pm or 8pm) although some close between 2pm and 4pm. The central post office is open from 8am to 10pm (see p. 34), and bars and clubs don't really begin to buzz until 1am in the morning (see p. 114), so serious clubbers will need a good lie-in to prepare for the long night ahead.

USEFUL ADDRESSES AND INFORMATION

SPANISH TOURIST OFFICES WORLDWIDE

UK & Ireland

22-23 Manchester Square
London W1M 5AP
☎ 020 7486 8077
📠 020 7486 8034

USA

666, 5th Avenue, 35th floor
New York NY 10103
☎ 212 265 8822

8383 Wilshire Blvd
Beverly Hills
Los Angeles CA 90211
☎ 213 658 7188

845 North Michigan Avenue
Chicago IL 60611
☎ 312 642 1992

1221 Brickell Avenue
Suite 1850
Miami FL 33131
☎ 305 358 1992

Australia and New Zealand

c/o Spanish Tour Promotions
178 Collins Street
Melbourne
☎ 03 9650 737

(For tourist offices in Barcelona, see page 33).

WEBSITES

There are some good websites with plenty of tourist information. Try:
www.tourspain.es
www.okspain.org

www.barcelonaturisme. com

The first two offer detailed practical information on the whole of Spain and Tourspain, the website of the Spanish Tourist Board, also offers detailed information on Barcelona. Meanwhile the Barcelona Turisme site is ideal for checking out the latest news and events before you go.
If you want to find out more while you're away, you can use the Internet for half an hour for €3.60 at:

Insolit
Maremagnum, local 111
(C3) ☎ 93 225 81 78
(see p. 119).

---

are entitled to basic health care in case of illness or accident. Make sure you obtain an E111 form (available from UK post offices), which will enable you to recover any medical expenses you may incur while on your trip. The *Barcelona Centro Medico* is responsible for helping foreign patients and will help with any medical problems and provide information on hospitals, doctors and dentists.

Barcelona Centro Medico
Avinguda Diagonal, 612, 2-14
☎ 93 930 34 64
☎ 639 30 34 64 (24hrs)
📠 93 414 04 57
www.bcm.es (in English and Spanish versions).

It's important to take out comprehensive travel insurance to cover theft, as pickpockets are common in the city and thieves are amazingly efficient. Paying for your trip by credit card may cover you for some medical assistance and lost luggage, so check with your credit card company before you leave.

A TASTE OF THE SUN AND THE MOUNTAINS

Like the country itself, Catalan cuisine has an authentic rustic flavour. The contrasting tastes of the Pyrenees and Mediterranean are combined in simple delicious dishes. Plain ingredients are simmered to conjure up substantial, nourishing fare, such as wild rabbit with prawns, beef stew with haricot beans, partridge with cabbage, cod with ratatouille, charcoal grilled snails with boletus mushrooms and many more designed to tempt the appetite with all the mouth-watering aromas of Catalonia.

THE BASIC INGREDIENTS: SAUCES AND *PA AMB TOMÀQUET*

Catalan cuisine is generally prepared with olive oil or lard and uses a few basic sauces. *Picada* is made from almonds, garlic, pine nuts, walnuts, hazelnuts, oil, stale bread, warm water and chopped parsley ground in a mortar. *Sofregit* is made from finely-chopped fried onions and tomato. *Samfain* is a

ratatouille made from peppers, aubergines, tomatoes and sometimes onions. *Ailloli* contains just garlic, oil and salt. Simple but irresistible *pa amb tomàquet* (bread and tomatoes) accompanies meals. It consists of a slice of toast rubbed with raw tomato and sprinkled with salt and a dash of olive oil (see **Casa Leopoldo**, p. 79).

A TASTE OF THE SUN IN WINTER

Escudella i carn d'olla is a tasty stew made from beef, pig's ears and trotters, poultry, lamb, black and white *botifares* sausages, cabbage, celery, carrots, turnips, potatoes and haricot beans. To these are added *pilota*, a mixture of minced pork and veal combined with white breadcrumbs, eggs and spices. It's a typical regional dish that's prepared on cold days and always served in the Christmas season.

MEDITERRANEAN FLAVOURS

With one foot in the country and the other on the coast, Catalans appreciate the produce of both the mountains and the Mediterranean. Aperitifs are served with shellfish *tapas* prepared with *tellines* and razor-shells (razor clams), fried red mullet and glass-eels, and grilled octopus and squid (see **Cal Pep**, p. 78). Or you can try *suquet de peix*, Costa Brava-style bouillabaisse, sea bream in a

CATALAN COOKING UTENSILS

If you long to emulate the locals in their cuisine, here are a few utensils you'll need to make tasty Catalan dishes successfully, together with the names of the shops where you can buy them. *Paella* dishes can be found at **Juan Soriano Raura** (see p. 99), while *olles*, the traditional olive and sand-coloured terracotta cooking pots, salamander irons and ramekins for *crema catalana* (crème brûlée), and *porrós*, glass jugs with long spouts for drinking the local Pénédès white wine, can all be found at **Caixa de Fang** (see p. 99).

salt crust, *daurada a la sal*, and *arros negre*, black rice in cuttlefish ink, at **Set Portes** (see p. 55) or in the shade of a vine on the Tibidabo hill (see p. 63).

branches and served with *ailloli*. In winter, the traditional *calçotada* unites family and friends round *calçots a la brasa*, leeks grilled over a wood fire, served with a sauce whose recipe is a closely-guarded secret. *Butifarra negra*, or black pudding, is made from lean pork mixed with pig's blood. *Butifarra de l'Empordà* is sweetened and flavoured with lemon peel and cinnamon using a recipe that dates back as far as the Middle Ages.

TEMPTING DESSERTS

Of all the many mouth-watering desserts – crisp biscuits, spiced cakes and fromage blanc coated with honey and almonds – there's one, *crema catalana* or *cremada*, that's irresistibly smooth (see **Granja Viader**, p. 80). This delicious crème brûlée flavoured with cinnamon is served with a misty glass of chilled *cava*. This local champagne is a speciality of the village of Sant Sadurni d'Anoia, where you can visit the Codorniù cellars in their magnificent *Modernista* setting.

THROUGHOUT THE YEAR

Catalonia is generous with its produce in every season and the Catalans are especially fond of *cargolades*, traditional country dishes made from snails and meat grilled on vine

COPAS, TAPAS AND THE REST

Barcelona is a city of cafés and bars. Some of them have already become the stuff of legend, while others are boldly avant-garde. In a city which boasts such a large variety of districts, each with its own distinctive character, you'll come across bars decorated with bric-a-brac, home-made distilleries with closely guarded secret recipes and *tapas* bars with ancient counters worn smooth by generations. There is something to suit everyone, from elderly domino players and veterans reliving past glories to the energetic and exuberant young.

ENTERTAINING CATALAN-STYLE

Catalans don't readily invite people to their homes. As in many Mediterranean countries, people go out to socialise. An invitation *anar de tasca* or *ir de tapas* is seen as a mark of trust. You spend the evening going from bar to bar, never to get drunk but to meet friends informally over tempting snacks and a glass of the local wine.

HOT AND SPICY

The word *tapas* is said to come from the covers that used to be placed over glasses of wine to stop flies falling in (*tapar* means to close or stop). Once a piece of ham or cheese had been placed on the top it was only a short step towards creating the *tapas* we know today. The *tapas* menu is hugely varied, from *escalivada*, pickled aubergines and peppers in olive oil, to fried octopus, and from anchovies to the *embotits* (sausages and hams) of the Pyrenees. *Fuets*, dry sausages, sausage with black pepper and *pernil serrano*, a local ham, will all be on the menu.

TAPAS ETIQUETTE

The *tapas* tradition is most firmly rooted in Andalusia and the Basque Country and takes a slightly different form in Catalonia. You order *a la barra* (at the bar), *de racìon* or *media racìon* (a portion or half-portion) a little before dinner time (see p. 8), and avoid raising your voice to distinguish yourself from Andalusians, whom the Catalans consider far too noisy. People usually pay for their own drinks, although you can of course buy a round, if you're feeling generous.

CHIRINGUITO AND *BODEGA*

A *bodega* is a wine bar or inn, often decorated with casks and barrels to add a touch of local colour. Drinks are served to order and it isn't uncommon for the wine list to also feature a selection of cold meats. The *Can* or *Casa* offers home

cooking, with produce fresh from the market simmering on the stove. The seafront *chiringuito* is a fishermen's restaurant, while the *fonda* is an inn where you eat whatever's in the pot. *Granjas* make delicious sweets from farm and dairy produce, while *horchaterias* specialise in barley water flavoured with almonds or tiger nuts, *horchata de chufa*.

IT COULD ONLY HAPPEN HERE...

All sorts of activities are available in bars across Barcelona, especially games such as *Manilla*, Catalan tarot or the card game *subhastat*.

Old men from the locality while the afternoon away using chickpeas or grains of corn as counters. Elsewhere there are fruit machines to lead you astray, though the **Nick Havanna** bar (see p. 118) has installed a book vending machine to salve your conscience. The restaurant **El Japones** (see p. 115), with its smart, minimalist interior, attracts a young, trendy crowd. But with French billiards already on offer at the **Velòdrom** (see p. 118), darts available elsewhere and Internet cafés springing up all over the city, there's always a quest for something different. One of the newer bars, **L'Arquer** (see p. 116), may

(see p. 118)

LE MARSELLA AND FRANCO'S DICTATORSHIP

The **Marsella's** (see p. 118) decor hasn't changed since it was founded in 1820 by a native of Marseilles as a place to drink absinthe. Since the turn of the century the Lamiel family have presided here. During the fascist dictatorship, singing and meetings were strictly forbidden in the bar, and the writing on the tarnished mirrors still reads *'està prohibido cantar'* (singing prohibited). If this somewhat decadent setting appeals to you, you can also have your cards read by a tarot expert.

have found the answer. It offers *copas y flechas,* which allows you to have a drink while brushing up on your archery skills (€7.20 for 30 minutes).

RELIGIOUS FESTIVALS AND TRADITIONS

Throughout the year, religious festivals and traditions turn the city into an open-air theatre. Popular culture is still very much alive, delighting crowds of onlookers with processions of papier-mâché giants. With Fellini-style cross-dressing at carnival time, interminable dancing of *sardanas* (see p.17) and amazing balancing acts by *castellers* (see p. 6), these festivals are a very lively sight indeed. Each celebration is accompanied by special sweets and cakes and the shop windows are full of colour. Barcelona is a festive city throughout the year.

DECEMBER

From 13 December onwards, Santa Llucia's (St Lucy's) Day, the cathedral square is covered with stalls on which tinsel, baubels, beads and ribbons evokes the atmosphere of Christmas. The crib figures are given a place of honour, displayed in a setting of bark and moss, but the presence of the *caganer* – a typical Catalan figure of a shepherd relieving himself – is a big surprise. He's supposed to be fertilising the ground and is thus a fertility symbol (you can buy crib figures at **Rosès**, see p. 92).

JANUARY

To celebrate New Year' Eve, family and friends gather to eat the *postre del music* (musician's dessert) made of honey, dried fruit and *matò* (curdled milk). On the stroke of midnight, everyone eats twelve grapes for good luck in time with the chimes. During the night of 5th to 6th January small children leave *turróns* and dried fruit for the Wise Men, along with bread and water for their camels. These same Wise Men disembark at the port for the *Cabalgata de los Reyes Magos* (the Procession of the Three Wise Men). This is the most magical time of all for the children. They have already written out their lists of longed-for presents and treats, having handed them in to one of the pages who were in the city a few days earlier. The Wise Men now hand out the presents, but naughty children are only given a lump of coal.

FEBRUARY

From Shrove Tuesday to Ash Wednesday the *Carnestoltes*, carnival celebrations, which were banned for a long time under Franco, take place.

MOSCATEL

Vallformosa

On the last day they burn the effigy of a character embodying the carnival. There are masked balls and processions of floats in the streets of the city as well as in Sitges (see p. 68). (You can buy fancy dress at **Menkes,** see p. 93, an Aladdin's cave full of wonderful creations.

MARCH

March 19 is San Josep's (St Joseph's) Day, patron saint of fathers and carpenters, and a very popular Christian name throughout Catalonia. It's celebrated by eating *crema catalana* (see p. 11, buy the necessary cooking utensils at **Caixa de Fang** see p. 99). Palm Sunday opens Holy Week and on Rambla de Catalunya, you can buy palm leaves woven into crosses, flowers, fantastic birds and so on. In the Mediterranean region, the palm tree is a symbol of regeneration and immortality On Easter Sunday godfathers give their godchildren a *mona*, a cake in the shape of a crown with several whole eggs set in it. The Easter egg represents life and perfection (buy them at **La Colmena** see p. 113).

APRIL

Along with England, Catalonia celebrates Sant Jordi's (Saint George's) Day on 23 April. The patron saint had his hour of glory in the Middle Ages, when he slayed a dragon. The Catalan nobility adopted him as their emblem when they recaptured Catalonia from the Moors. On this day, a lover gives his sweetheart a rose and she in return gives him a book (**Sant Jordi** book-shop, see p. 111).

MAY

On 11 May, the fair of Sant Ponç, patron saint of homeopaths, is a chance to buy medicinal and aromatic herbs. On Carrer de l'Hospital, stalls and stands are set up selling delicious syrups, candied fruit and honey to the delight of the sweet-toothed. Barcelona still has around forty herbalist's shops with fragrant window displays dotted about the different areas of the city (see **Anormis** p. 39).

JUNE

In June, *Corpus Christi* celebrates the Eucharist. Since 1264, Christianity has taken over ancient processions designed to ripen the corn, and *caps grossos* ('big heads' and giants) parade through the streets. In Barcelona, the tradition of the *ou com balla* (dancing egg) has taken place in the cathedral cloisters and patio of the Casa del Ardiaca since the 18th century. An empty egg is balanced on the jet of the fountain. For some people this symbolic association of water and birth has a profound

religious significance. The 23 June is St John's Eve, when the summer solstice is celebrated with bonfires. In the past, people used to burn old objects and furniture at crossroads, as a sign of

purification. Nowadays this is no longer allowed, except on Montjuïc Hill. Passing three times over the flames is said to protect you from evil and people share *coca*, pine-kernel cake sprinkled with *barreja*, a mixture of malmsey, muscatel and spirits.

JULY AND AUGUST

During the summer months, the famous *castells* are erected, and every Catalan dreams of becoming a *casteller* of his town. The 'castell' is the symbol of the community. For the townspeople, it means building a living castle by balancing one on top of another. Several volunteers form a muscular base onto which the rest climb. Groups compete to reach from five to nine levels. It's always a child, the *anxaneta*, who sets out to conquer the castle and waves to the crowd when he reaches the top. This Mediterranean tradition originated in ceremonies

designed to celebrate the earth's fertility. On 15 August the festival of Gràcia starts and for around two weeks there's drinking and dancing in the streets of the former village,

which is now part of Barcelona. The people of Barcelona are extremely proud of their local traditions.

SEPTEMBER

Catalonia's National Day (*Diada*) falls on 11 September and commemorates the taking of Barcelona by Felipe V in 1714. Local institutions were then abolished and the day has become the symbol of nationalism. It's not the defeat of the city that's being celebrated, but the fight against the Bourbons. There's a good deal of Catalan Flag waving on the *Diada*. On 24 September, the *Festes de la Mercè* are dedicated to the

Virgin Mary, who was made the patron saint of Barcelona in the 19th century. Since then, she's headed the bill at the *Festa Major*, when the city's inhabitants are in a kind of ferment, both secular and religious. Delicious local produce is on offer on every street corner, while giants and dragons drive out evil spirits. During the week of 24 September people attend musical and theatrical performances in the Sant Jaume, Cathedral and del Rei squares, Plaça Reial and Escorxador Park.

NOVEMBER

All Saints' Day puts an end to the autumn festivities and celebration of abundance. Now it's time to remember the dead and turn fearsome beings into benevolent ancestors. In former times, on the eve of All Saints' Day, families would gather together to say rosaries for the dead while eating sweet chestnuts. The thick consistency of the chestnuts was supposed to block the way to roaming spirits, which people feared would try to take over the bodies of the living. Nowadays, you merely eat *panellets*, marzipan sweets covered in pine nuts in memory of the chestnuts, accompanied by a sweet wine.

THE CATALONIAN LOCAL DANCE, THE *SARDANA*

The *sardana*, the quintessential Catalan dance, has very ancient, probably Cretan, origins. All generations take part in it and, after a brief introductory step, short eight-bar steps alternate with long sixteen-bar ones, repeated twice over. At the end, the dancers join hands in the centre of the circle. The band, or *cobla*, consists of eleven musicians playing the *flabiol* (a recorder played with one hand), the tambourine, two cornets, a *fiscorn*, two *tibles* (wind instruments) and the *tenora* (oboe), the instrument that symbolises the *sardana*. You can join in the dancing on Sundays at noon in the cathedral square and at 6.30pm in Sant Jaume Square (and you can buy your espadrilles for dancing at **Manual Alpargatera**, see p. 87).

A FOOTBALL CRAZY CITY

With the unifying slogan 'More than a club', the legendary football team Barça has the loyalty of some 105,000 members, more than any other football club in the world. When Barça wins, flags fly, horns sound and there's singing in the streets. And if you casually mention the magic word Barça when talking to a Catalan, you'll score an immediate hit and any wariness will vanish in a flash.

THE BARÇA FOOTBALL CLUB

The club was founded in 1899, when Barcelona had aspirations of becoming an important capital. The Great Exhibition of 1888 had launched the city on its way and it was trying to become part of the European movement. Over a century has passed since the Swiss, Hans Gamper, founded this local institution. It's amusing to think that Barça, a symbol of the Catalan spirit, wears the red and blue of a Swiss province, and that the majority of the founder members were English or German.

A SPIRIT OF INDEPENDENCE

Barça's matches against Real Madrid under Franco were a focus for the hatred of centralism. Its financial strength – it's the richest club in Europe, with an annual budget of 31 million euros – and political attitude under the dictatorship constantly attracted enmity. Nowadays it remains the bastion of the Catalan spirit, combined with a desire to cross the Pyrenees in search of international recognition.

FROM NORTH TO SOUTH

As Gamper named the club after the city, the people of Barcelona feel a great affinity with their football team. The club has been instrumental in the integration of 'immigrants' from other parts of Spain. To be a *socio* (member) is in a way to become Catalan, by affiliation to a winning side. From the start, the founders regarded the institution as a place of union and fraternity. It brings together people from every walk of life and membership cards are handed down from father to son.

NOU CAMP

Inaugurated in September 1957, Nou Camp replaced the original and legendary Corts Stadium. A single stone from Corts Stadium became the foundation stone of the new stadium, thus ensuring

continuity. Designed by three architects, Soteras, Mitjans and Barbòn, it can hold 120,000 spectators and is the second largest stadium in the world.

THE FOUNTAIN OF CANALETES

There's a place in Barcelona at the top of the Ramblas where people

gather to talk about sport. The Fountain of Canaletes, on the site of an ancient spring, was once the meeting-

place of strangers passing through the city. Nowadays it's where the latest match against Real Madrid is discussed and football takes on the air of a medieval joust. If you read a little Castilian Spanish buy a local daily, *la Vanguardia* or *el Periodico*, and, to complete the picture, dip into the famous novel by Manuel Vázquez Montalbán, *'Offside'* (published by Bourgois). At this rate, you'll soon be one of the four million Catalans who won't go to bed on Sunday without first having found out the Barça results!

THE BARÇA CLUB SONG

A whole stadium filled with supporters is always an impressive sight and the Nou Camp echoing with the club song makes Barça a force to be reckoned with.
'We are the reds and blues *(la gente blaugrana)*.
It doesn't matter where we come from,
North or South,
On this we all agree,
We're brothers under the flag,
Red and blue in the wind.
A cry of courage has made our name known throughout the world – Barça, Barça, Barça!'

ANTIQUES AND OLD LACE

Barcelona has a good choice of antiques shops and markets, so those who enjoy strolling around its narrow streets and ancient squares stand a chance of finding something interesting.

A diligent search can uncover old *azulejos*, ceramics, cooking utensils, a betrothal chest *(caixa de nùvia),* or even an old edition of Tintin in Catalan. The flea market, Els Encants, is a good source for finds. It has a colourful sea of stalls with a mixture of old clothes and bric-a-brac.

CATALAN FURNITURE

From the Middle Ages onwards, Catalonia was linked to the rest of Europe by sea. Overland transport remained more difficult, and furniture from the rest of Spain seldom found its way into the region. It was as rare to own a Spanish cabinet in Cordovan morocco, a *bargueno*, as it was a Chinese vase. Instead, furniture and other goods were imported from other countries such as England and France.

AN AIR OF PROVENCE

In times gone by, carpenters from Provence settled in Girona and passed on secrets of their trade. You'll come across a great deal of this *masia* (farmhouse) furniture made of walnut, sometimes inlaid with light boxwood. Often, for reasons of economy, the front of the furniture was elaborately worked, while the back was left rough. Over the centuries carpenters worked in oak, walnut, silver birch, poplar and even mahogany imported from overseas.

THE *CAIXA DE NUVIA*

The betrothal chest was an institution in Catalan families from the 16th to the 18th century. Generally made of walnut, it was around 140cm/55in long and 60cm/24in high and was used

for storage. It spread from the plains to the mountains and became common in both farmhouses and palaces. On their wedding day, the betrothed couple were each given a chest containing their dowry. The woman's had a small door, which opened to reveal a jewel compartment. In the 18th century, this traditional chest gave way to a chest of drawers, then a mirrored wardrobe, less mobile, but more practical for storing belongings.

FROM ANTIQUES TO AZULEJOS

Antique lovers should make their way to the Call, the old ghetto of medieval Barcelona (see p. 39). The streets of Banys Nous and Paja are lined with

antique shops. At 8 Paja, they sell a fine selection of walking sticks with ivory, mother-of-pearl and silver knobs, as well as sumptuous ostrich-feather fans and vases made of glass similar in style to that of Gallé. At 11 Paja, Erika Niedermaier (see p. 103) sells delicate 17th-century ceramics with metallic detail, apothecaries' ointment pots and a wide variety of wrought-iron objects, whose history this devoted collector will be only too pleased to tell you. At 22 Banys Nous, Maria José Royo (see p. 103) specialises in sacred art, gilded wood, popular sculpture, and interesting and unusual Baroque liturgical objects. At 14 Banys Nous, there are items of early Catalan furniture, betrothal chests and lovely old *azulejos* (a word derived from the Persian *'al zuleich'*, meaning a smooth flat stone), colourful enamelled tiles typical of the Iberian Peninsula (see p. 103).

see p. 103; see p. 103; see p. 103; see p. 39; see p. 103

L'ARCA DE L'AVIA, THE STUFF OF DREAMS

C. dels Banys Nous, 20
☎ 93 302 15 98
Open Mon.-Fri. 10am-2pm, 5-8pm, Sat. 10am-2pm.

Founded in 1840, these famous suppliers to the Spanish royal family made bobbin lace and Spanish *mantillas*. At that time, such delicate accessories were highly prized and, as with jewellery, the amount a woman wore was a sign of her wealth. This shop is a treasure chest (*arca*) of everything that once made up a bride's trousseau – embroidered linen tablecloths and sheets, damask bath towels and even the ceremonial cloth in which the dowry was sometimes placed.

MODERNISME – EXUBERANCE AND EXTRAVAGANCE ABOVE ALL

Barcelona is renowned for its superb *Modernista* architecture. From the Palau de la Música and hospital of San Pau to the Quatre Gats bar and Bolòs pharmacy, this artistic movement shaped houses like sculptures, covered façades with azure and gold, and added floral designs to chimneys. Everything defies logic and order, and imagination rules supreme. On every street corner, you come face to face with the spirit of inventiveness and unusual detail that makes this city so fascinating.

A FAMILY LIKENESS

Modernisme refers to a cultural movement that emerged at the end of the 19th century. It had similarities with the British Modern Style, Belgian 1900 Style, German Jugendstil, Viennese and Prague Sezessionstil, Italian Liberty and French Art Nouveau. It became famous because of its appropriation of the powerful *Renaixença* (1878), or the movement for a return to the Catalan identity. Writers, musicians and poets added their efforts to those of painters and architects to turn Modernisme into a lifestyle.

AT THE TURN OF THE CENTURY

In the 19th century, people believed that progress and science would be the saviours of humanity. However, at the turn of the century, this thinking underwent a serious crisis, triggering anarchy and assassination attempts, and Barcelona was nick-named 'The Rose of Fire'. Subjectivity, irrationality, a return to nature and oriental doctrines overtook order and reason. Modernisme was a reaction to academicism and provincial bad taste. Sustained by the profits of industrialisation and commerce, Modernisme found patrons in the wealthy inhabitants of Barcelona.

THE ROOTS OF CATALAN ART

The desire to return to its origins was rooted in the desire to review the glories of the Catalonia's past and her achievements. In England, at the same time as this, the Pre-Raphelite Brotherhood (1848), the Arts and Crafts Movement (1888) and Symbolism were promoting spiritual art with a social purpose. The designer William Morris (1864-1896) relaunched the craft industry taking inspiration from nature, while in France Viollet-le-Duc (1814-1879) became fascinated by medieval bulidings.

HOW TO RECOGNISE THE *MODERNISTA* STYLE

In the 19th century, eclectic architecture dominated the scene and buildings were a mixture of styles. They could display Egyptian, Roman, Moorish and Greco-Roman influences, as the university, (see p. 52), while the neo-Gothic style was also an unqualified success. *Modernista* architects distinguished themselves by the use they made of these sources of inspiration. Sinuous lines, asymmetry, dynamism, richness of detail and refinement were all of great importance.

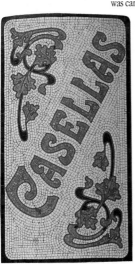

FROM STREET LIGHTS TO SHOP SIGNS

Modernisme regarded a design as a 'total work' integrating all the arts. It could be the result of collaboration between cabinetmakers, craftsmen in mosaics, ceramicists, jewellers, craftsmen in wrought iron, sculptors and master glass makers, all driven by attention to detail. From door handles to mosaic cladding, everything was carefully designed. Take a look at the hallways of *Modernista* buildings and appreciate the wealth of decorative detail used.

KEEPING THE LADIES HAPPY

Barcelona still has some two hundred shops and clothing stores dating from this era, which were designed with women very much in mind. You can picture elegant ladies, dressed in velvet or damask choosing fabric for a new outfit, or selecting from the very latest,

IN PURSUIT OF MODERNISME

Wake up and have breakfast at the Hotel **España** (see p. 75). Go for a walk and shop for delicious chocolates at **Antiga Casa Figueras** (see p. 49), rare stamps from **Monge** (see p. 104), and made-to-measure shirts at **Xancò** (see p. 48). Take a leisurely lunch on the terrace of **El Asador de Aranda** (see p. 78) or in the more formal setting of **Dama**. In the afternoon, visit the **Museu d'Art Modern de Catalunya** (see p. 55) and stop for a coffee at **Hivernacle** (see p.80), pop into the **Palau Macaya** (see p. 107) for a temporary exhibition, and in the evening go to a concert at the **Palau de la Música** (see pp. 40 and 123), or to **Almirall** for a drink (see p. 119).

fashionable accessories. Some women would tie their ankles together in order not to tear the delicate fabric of their tight skirts, so it would appear that being a fashion victim is by no means a new thing…

TOTAL DESIGN

'Make Barcelona beautiful', the slogan of the 1990s, triggered an avalanche of innovative projects. Barcelona wanted to improve its appearance, and exploring it on foot, you'll discover open-air sculptures, smart traffic signs and state-of-the-art phone booths that amount to a kind of street art. From comic strips to coathangers, nothing escapes this creative fever, and modern designs and the traditional Catalan identity combine to stunning effect.

AN ANCESTRAL TRADITION

Catalonia is at the cutting edge of Spanish design, but why here more than elsewhere? When the New World was discovered Catalans were harassed out of any form of trade with the Americas whatsoever. They never profited from the crock of gold which the Americas became and so devoted all their efforts to developing their own strengths and resources. The result of this inward concentration of effort was a strong tradition of family cottage industries which have lasted throughout the centuries.

IDEAS, BUT NO RAW MATERIALS

Like all countries lacking in raw materials (Japan, Sweden, Switzerland, etc.), Catalonia specialised in light manufacturing – textiles, glass, ceramics, leather, metallurgy, wood, paper and the graphic arts. *Modernisme* (see p. 22) advocated the idea of the 'total work', arguing that an architect ought to be able to produce the whole design, both outside and inside. This concept of symbiosis between raw materials and interior design was revived in the 1950s by the generation of architects that included Oriol Bohigas, Josep Antoni Coderch and designers such as André Ricard and Oscar Tusquets.

THE DESIGNERS – JACKS-OF-ALL TRADES

It isn't easy to classify the artists who move from one discipline to another – from architecture to interior design, by way of

Turn-of-the-century furniture by Gaudí

fashion, ceramics and even graphics. Most representative of them all is perhaps Xavier Mariscal, the prodigious young designer of ceramics, posters, comic strips, wardrobes, shoes, and carpets. His mascot for the Olympic Games, 'Cobi', has become an international star just as its creator.

DESIGN ORGANISATIONS

After forty years of Francoism the city has one more taken up its creative vocation. Today there are seven schools of design, and many design bodies. The oldest and most prestigious organisation is the FAD (Foundation of the Decorative Arts), which awards an annual prize to the best designer. Caixa, one of the biggest Spanish banks, is an outstanding contributor, providing ever-present support for science and the arts, continuing a very Catalan turn-of-the-century tradition of patronage (see the Güells, pp. 30-31). In addition to this,

every two years in April, the city organises a 'Design Spring', a tour of galleries, shops and bars to make sure its inhabitants are ready for all the latest trends when the good weather starts. For more information, call ☎ 93 218 28 22.

CATALAN SPECIALITIES

If you want to get into Catalan design, there's plenty of choice – formal furniture or crazy lamps by Mariscal and Cortès, an armchair with a 'Mantis' wooden shell by Pep Bonnet, Mariscal furnishing fabric by Marietta or his 'duplex' stool with colourful wavy feet. More sober and timeless is the TMC lamp (1961) by Milà exhibited at the MoMA, or the Lluscà pressure cooker. All these designs have the distinctive feature of playing with different styles and influences (especially Italian) to invent a brand new style of their own, involving a concern for detail, materials and humour, and producing enormously creative designs.

FASHIONABLE DESIGNERS

Barcelona has always had a reputation as being a haven for artists, and this is still as true as ever. Gaudì and Mariscal are well known names, but few people have heard of the city's new young designers. It's as if those outside Barcelona still think design here is frozen in the 1980s. Nothing could be further from the truth – the city is buzzing with innovative, unique and often surprising examples of creativity.

SEARCHING FOR AUTHENTICITY

The 1980s saw a real creative boom in Barcelona. Design was the new watchword of the city, and conversations invariably began with the question: 'Are you a designer or do you have a real job?' The 1990s saw a marked move towards a more honest interpretation of design, which gradually became authentic rather than trendy, minimal rather than complicated and far more accessible to the general public. The use of natural materials and simple lines and forms became the order of the day.

UNIQUE JEWELLERY CREATIONS

If you are tired of the usual gold bangles, pearl necklaces and paste earrings that you find in most jewellers, then you may find the creations of the new Barcelona designers more interesting. **Karin Wagner** creates unusual pieces in lightweight felt. Her earrings and rings, produced in a range of subtle

colours, are quite stunning. **Ana Hagopian** is yet another champion of unusual materials. Her pieces are real works of art, made from folded recycled paper, glued, cut and painted by hand. **Chelo Sastre**'s jewellery is made using rather more classic materials, but still

based on recycled products. She has spent many years refining her designs, which are soft and sensuous. **Clara Uslé** also deserves a mention after the successful launch of her first collection in 1999. She has become a master at applying colour and motifs onto silver and gold.

COSY INTERIORS

Lovers of interior design will be seduced by the creations of various newcomers on the Barcelona scene. Simplicity is the key once more, in a range of items such as cutlery, crockery and home furnishings. **Nani Marquina**'s rugs combine form, texture and colour and are both elegant and contemporary in design. **Estudi Eulalia Coma** produces wonderful crockery, particularly the Blau Pics range with the patterns concentrated around the edge. Today's young artists have also

not forgotten the children. **Virginia Pulm**'s pieces are decorated with patterns that look as if they have been designed not only with children in mind but by the children themselves.

STYLISH AND ELEGANT CLOTHES

Fashion designers don't just clothe women, they pay homage to them with creations in silk, velvet, linen and pure cotton. **Lydia Delgado**, a former classical ballet dancer from Liceu, is now one of the top designers

in Barcelona. **Ruth**, on the other hand, is focussing her talents (for the moment, anyway) on children's clothing. Her simple embroidered motifs are based on the natural world – insects, animals and plants – and are quite unique.

ANTONIO MIRÓ

Antonio Miró has been dressing both men and women for 25 years, so why place him in this category of young designers? Every season Antonio reinvents himself, constantly reinterpreting

classic fashion designs. His clothes are well cut, impeccably finished, simple but stylish and produced in natural fabrics. His attention to detail distinguishes him from the rest of the crowd.

WHERE TO FIND TODAY'S DESIGNERS

Karin Wagner
Forum (see p. 86).

Lydia Delgado
See p. 87.

Antonio Miró
See p. 53.

Chelo Sastre
At Hipòtesi (see p. 89), La Pedrera (see p. 51), Moska (see p. 43) and Pilma (see below).

Nani Marquina
Pilma, C. de València, 1
☎ 93 226 06 93.

Clara Uslé
At MNAC (see p. 66) and the Fondació Joan Miró (see p. 66).

Ana Hagopian
At Forum (see p. 86), Cromía (see p. 98), Hipòtesi (see p. 89) and Moska (see p. 43).

Virginia Pulm
At Vinçon (see p. 52).

Estudi Eulalia Coma
At Vinçon (see p. 52).

Ruth
Biscuit, Passeig de Gràcia Rambla Cataluña, 66
☎ 93 215 81 70
(for more information call the showroom on
☎ 93 488 14 00.

MIRÓ, PICASSO AND TÀPIES

Barcelona is synonymous with the genius of three great artists, Miró, Picasso and Tàpies. Each in turn was inspired to produce images of the city in keeping with his own particular vision. Miró transformed the world into a riot of colours and shapes, Picasso sketched locals and peasants with just a few strokes, while Tàpies experimented with collage and engraving techniques.

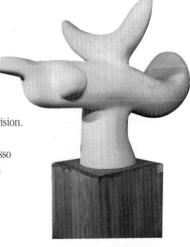

monuments bearing his signature. To complete your whirlwind study you can also see exhibits of his work at the **Museu de Ceràmica** (see p. 62) and then try a cocktail at **Boadas** (see p. 48), a bar which he regularly frequented.

JOAN MIRÓ

Born in 1893 in a small street in the heart of the Ciutat Vella (Old Town), Miró always remained very attached to Catalonia. He became an artist of international renown, but never forgot his homeland. His first exhibition was held in 1918 after which he divided his time between Spain and France. The **Fondació Joan Miró** (p. 66) is a good way to see his work. Look for sculptures, lithographs, etchings, tapestries, ceramics, theatre sets and masks. The city is littered with

PABLO PICASSO

Born in Malaga, Picasso was barely fourteen years old when he arrived in Barcelona in 1895. He lived here for seven years before settling in Paris in 1904. His formative years were spent in a turn-of-

Pablo Picasso, Les Demoiselles d'Avignon.

the-century climate much influenced by Modernisme (see p. 22). His studies of the Barceloneta, the dissident fringes of the Barrio Chino and his first Blue Period works (**Museu Picasso**, see p. 40), reflect the misery pervading the Barcelona of 1900. He lived with his parents in the Plaça de la Mercè and studied at the **Llotja** Art School (see p. 42). Later he took a flat at 36 Nou de la Rambla and frequented the variety cafés of the Barrio Chino or

The Carrer d'Avinyó.

El Raval, the city's red light district. The title of his famous painting *Les Demoiselles d'Avignon* (1906) was inspired by a brothel in the Carrer d'Avinyó frequented by sailors from the neighbouring port.

ANTONI TÀPIES

It's difficult to separate the life and work of this artist born in 1923. All his creativity was channelled towards the service of the political. He was influenced by the Dadaist and Surrealist movements and turned his art into a free-thinking, provocative game. He developed an abstract style

which looked deceptively simple, including the use of symbols as a kind of sign language, and incorporating every day objects in his work. Tàpies produced his first major pieces in 1945. For a thorough appreciation of

QUATRE GATS CAFÉ
C. Montsiò, 3
☎ **93 302 41 40**
Closed Sun. lunchtime.

This café opened in 1897, on the ground floor of a neo-Gothic building designed by the *Modernista* architect Puig i Cadafalch. The name 'Quatre Gats' is probably a tribute to the Chat Noir (Black Cat), a Parisian cabaret that Pere Romeu, one of the founders of the Quatre Gats, knew from having worked there. From 1897 to 1903, the Quatre Gats saw gatherings of the artists and writers of the day. Picasso designed the menu and held his first exhibition here in 1900.

this unique artist visit the **Fundacio Antoni Tàpies** (see p. 51). Then visit **Ediciones T** (see p. 107), the art gallery founded in 1994 by his son, which specialises in graphic works and books. It also makes a point of exhibiting young Catalan and foreign talent.

GAUDÍ:
UTOPIA WITH
A HEART

Antoni Gaudí is an architect inseparable from our image of Barcelona. Both visionary and iconoclast, he is the embodiment of this surprising and intoxicating city. Born in 1852, he was a fervent nationalist and misanthropist, and very devout. Towards the end of the century, with the cultural and political rebirth and a new economic prosperity, the enlightened middle classes were eager to adopt the new European trends and Gaudí profited particularly from the patronage of Eusebio Güell.

PARC GÜELL

Between 1900 and 1914, Gaudí wanted to create a garden along the lines of an English park, as a contrast to the growing industrialisation of the city. His sponsor, Eusebi Güell (see box opposite) was preoccupied with utopian social reforms. The area was originally barren and Gaudí

refused to have the ground levelled and subjected his designs to the demands of the landscape. Slanting supporting columns make the paths look more like tunnels. (To reach Parc Güell, take the metro to Vallcara, walk to the open-air escalator and ride to the top.)

CHAMELEON-LIKE
ARCHITECTURE

At times, confusion sets in and it's hard to tell where Gaudí's designs begin and where nature ends. His work merges, chameleon-like, with the very ground on which it is built. Gaudí drew inspiration from many sources, but beneath an apparently haphazard exterior, his work is very well-planned, and the fantastic shapes were designed with the help of detailed models. The area was

supposed to have been divided up into sixty parcels of land for housing, but only two were ever built, one of which is now the Gaudí museum. The project was never completed as Güell was afraid it would eat up his entire fortune. Today, the two houses at the entrance to the park look like ginger-bread houses, strange palaces built from odds and ends – hallucinogenic mushrooms with Moorish outlines and bold mosaics.

THE GÜELL FAMILY

Juan Antonio Güell used to boast that all the 'good families' of turn-of-the-century Barcelona came to his house in Pedralbes — aristocrats, the wealthy upper middle-classes, the 'nouveaux riches' and *indianos* with legendary fortunes. The latter group, to which the Güell family belonged, symbolised success, social climbing and prestige in the Spanish colonies. On their return to the city, they started a textile business and built palaces and parks. Eusebi Güell, the son of the founder of the line, became Antoni Gaudí's patron and commissioned many projects from him.

SUCCESSFUL INTEGRATION

Further into the park a multicoloured salamander stands guard, whilst at the top a square edged by a long

winding bench, with backrests in the shape of the human form overlooks the city. Josep Maria Jujol, Gaudí's assistant, collaborated with him on the project. They used broken ceramics as decoration reviving the Arab tradition of *azulejos* and thus preceding

the Dadaist and Cubist collages. Whatever your artistic preferences, a walk through this amazing park is a must. There is nothing like it anywhere else in the world (Carretera Carmel ☎ 93 284 64 46. Every day 10am-6pm in winter, 9am-8pm in summer).

LA SAGRADA FAMÍLIA

The first stone of this church dedicated to the Holy Family was laid in 1883. Like the Sacré-Coeur in Paris, it was built with the help of donations from the public. Its design and building occupied Gaudí for forty years. Sadly only the east façade depicting the life of Christ was finished before Gaudí's untimely death in 1926, when he was killed by a tram.

Unfortunately in 1936 all Gaudí's plans were destroyed by the Anarchists and so his designs could never be carried through to completion. However, work began once more towards the end of the 1950s, causing great controversy, and still continues to this day under the watchful eye of Jordi Bonet. This building is an exuberant flight of fantasy. Eight towers twist upwards into the sky, an extravaganza in stone which everyone can appreciate for its boldness and uniqueness, no matter what their individual tastes and preferences may be. Another 'must' on your visit to the city. (C. Mallorca, 401 ☎ 93 207 30 31, fax 93 476 10 10. Open every day 9am-6pm in winter, 9am-8pm in summer. Entry charge.)

What to see Practicalities

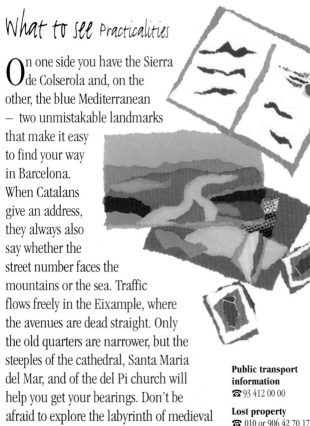

On one side you have the Sierra de Colserola and, on the other, the blue Mediterranean — two unmistakable landmarks that make it easy to find your way in Barcelona. When Catalans give an address, they always also say whether the street number faces the mountains or the sea. Traffic flows freely in the Eixample, where the avenues are dead straight. Only the old quarters are narrower, but the steeples of the cathedral, Santa Maria del Mar, and of the del Pi church will help you get your bearings. Don't be afraid to explore the labyrinth of medieval alleyways in the old town – you won't get lost for long and it's the best way to really get to know the place. So go ahead – a fascinating city lies in wait for you!

GETTING AROUND BARCELONA

Visit the old quarters (Raval, Ribera, and Gòtico) on foot and stroll around them at your leisure. The Eixample, criss-crossed by a network of wide avenues, is served by a number of bus routes and metro stations. The numerous taxis are among the cheapest in the European Union. You'll need them for going to the Güell Park and the Sagrada Familia, which are not in the city centre.

Public transport information
☎ 93 412 00 00

Lost property
☎ 010 or 906 42 70 17

Guardia Urbana
This is a service reserved for tourists in the event of theft, accident or loss of documents: La Rambla, 43
☎ 93 344 13 00
Open in the winter from 7am to midnight and in the summer from 7am to 2pm.

THE METRO
Air-conditioned and clean, it runs from Monday to Thursday from 5am to 11pm, on Friday and Saturday until 1am, and on Sunday from 6am to midnight. This is the

BY BIKE OR ROLLER BLADES

At weekends, Barcelona residents frequently hire bikes or roller blades to ride or skate along the waterfront or Diagonal. It's the ideal place for cycling enthusiasts and those who enjoy unusual walks. The place to go to hire a bike is opposite the Francià station: **Bicitram** Av. Marquès de Argentera, 15, ☎ 93 792 28 41. Open Sat., Sun. and public holidays. You can hire two-wheelers for €2.10 an hour here. Bike hire is also available on the Diagonal near the Corte Inglès, and at the Vila Olimpica.

fastest form of transport in Barcelona. In addition there are a few FGC (Ferro-carrils de la Generalitat de Catalunya) suburban city rail lines which link up with the metro, the most useful of which goes to the Tibidabo. Signs with the letter 'M' in a red diamond indicate the entrance to the metro stations. Signs for RENFE or FGC indicate a link with the national railway system or the Catalonian system. Tickets cost €0.84, but for the duration of your stay it's worth buying a T1 ticket (€4.66), which

entitles you to 10 journeys by bus and metro. You're restricted to travelling on the metro with the T2 ticket. In addition, there are 1-day (€3.46), 3-day (€8.11) and 5-day (€12.02) travel passes for bus and metro.

The 3 and 5-day passes can be bought in the commercial department of the Universitat station, Monday to Friday 8am to 8pm. Important intersections on these lines are Passeig de Gràcia, Catalunya, and Diagonal.

BUSES

Numerous bus lines cover the whole city. Buses operate from 6.30am to 10pm, and some continue right through to 4am. (Nitbus). You can tell which are which by their numbers and can consult the maps on bus shelters that give details of their routes. The Tomb bus is the most useful; it goes from Catalunya square to Pius XII square. Although more expensive, it runs every 5 to 10 minutes. Finally, there's a Tibibus that takes you from Catalunya square to Tibidabo square Saturday

and Sunday throughout the year, and every day in July and August, from 10.30am to 8.30pm; it's ideal if you want to visit the Tibidabo amusement park.

BY CAR

If you rent a car for the weekend, be very careful about where you park it. It will cost you €90 to free it from the city car pound. When you do find a space, which is not easy, don't leave any valuables in sight as thefts are common-place. Daytime car parks are reasonably safe (around €1.50 per hour, €18 a day).

Avis
Arago, 235
☎ 93 487 87 54,
🄵 93 487 20 50 or
☎ 93 478 17 06 (at airport).

Europcar
Consell
de Cent, 363,
☎ 93 488 21 92
🄵 93 488 23 98.

Hertz
Tuset, 8
☎ 93 217 32 48,
🄵 93 217 80 76.

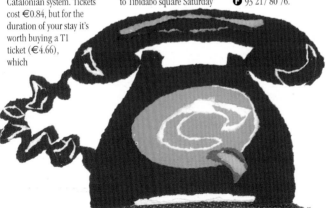

TAXIS

The city is swarming with 11,000 yellow and black taxis. The green light shows they're available. They are still very reasonable and rarely refuse to take you, even for very short distances. Over 1,000 taxis even accept credit cards. Allow €1.80 for picking up, then €0.65 per km/0.5mile. A supplement is charged for luggage, airport transfers and animals .

Barnataxi
☎ 93 357 77 55.

Taxi Radio Movil
☎ 93 358 11 11.

Radio Taxi
☎ 93 225 00 00.

BY TRAIN

To get to Sitges (see p. 68), take a train from Passeig de Gràcia station (RENFE station) or Sants station. Air-conditioned trains operate every 15 minutes from 6am to 11pm. and the journey to this charming seaside resort takes 35 minutes. Don't forget to date stamp your ticket, other-wise you risk getting fined!

MAKING A PHONE CALL

The international country code for Spain is 34. The code for Barcelona is 93. When dialling a local number from within Barcelona you must also ensure that you dial this 93 at the beginning – the codes were changed in 1998, making the old seven digit numbers nine digits. All the numbers in Spain now have nine digits and you dial all nine from wherever you are calling.

Public telephone booths have a distinctive modern design and are blue and green in colour. Calls are very expensive, and you'll never have enough coins to make an international call. It's much better to buy a phone card (for €6-12), at a tobacconist's.

Failing this, try the **locutorios telefonicos**, pay-phones installed at La Rambla, 88, open every day 10am-11pm, and at Sants station, open Mon.-Sat. 8am-10.30pm, Sun. 9am-10.30pm.

WRITING HOME

Oficina Central
Pl. Antoni Lopez,
☎ 90 219 71 97/93 318 30 48
Metro Barceloneta or Jaume I.
Open Mon.-Sat. 8.30am-9.30pm, Sun. and holidays 8.30am-2.30pm.

The impressive main post office is situated at the lower end of the Via Laietana. To send a postcard within Europe costs €0.42, and a postcard or letter weighing up to 20gm costs €0.72 to USA or Canada and €1.10 to Australasia. You can buy stamps from *estanques* or a tobacconist's. Letterboxes (mailboxes) are easy to spot – they're large with yellow lettering and are found at crossroads.

BUREAUX DE CHANGE

Banks are open Monday to Friday from 8.30am to 2pm, Saturday from 8.30am to 1pm (closed in summer).

American Express
Passeig de Gràcia, 101,
☎ 93 217 00 70
Open Mon.-Fri. 9.30am-6pm, Sat. 10am-noon.

Foreign currency can be changed every day at the airport at **Banco Exterior de España** from 7.30am to 10.45pm, and every day at Sants station from 8am to 10pm (except 1 and 6 January; and 25 and 26 December). The same applies in the city centre, at the offices of:

Exact Change
Av. Catedral, 1 and
La Rambla, 130.
Open every day 9am-10pm.

Cheque Point
La Rambla, 64.
Open every day 9am-midnight.

TOURIST INFORMATION OFFICES

Turisme de Barcelona
Pl. Catalunya, 17 (basement)
☎ 93 368 97 30
www.barcelonaturisme.com
email:
teltur@barcelonaturisme.com
Open every day 9am-9pm.

This is Barcelona's central tourist information office, which provides cultural information on the city, as well as hotel information and bookings and a bureau de change. Travelcards and phonecards are also on sale here and theatre and concert tickets can be bought from Caixa Catalunya in the information office.

Once you start exploring the city, you'll find that there are several other tourist offices dotted around Barcelona where you can also pick up maps, brochures and information (ask especially for brochures on Miró, *Modernisme*, Gaudí, New Urbanism and Quadrat d'Or).

At the airport:
Aeropuerto del Prat,
08820 Barcelona
☎ 93 478 05 65
(Terminals A and B)
Open every day 9am-9pm.

At Sants station:
Pl. de Països Catalans,
L'Estació de Sants
08014 – Barcelona
☎ 93 411 81 89
In winter open Mon.-Fri.
8am-8pm, Sat., Sun. and
public holidays 8am-2pm.
In summer, open every day
8am-8pm.

Pl. Sant Jaume:
(Ground floor of City Hall
in the Gothic Quarter)
Open Mon.-Sat. 10am-8pm,
Sun. and holidays 10am-2pm.

On the Ramblas:
Palau de la Virreina,
La Rambla, 99
☎ 93 301 77 75
Open Mon.-Sat. 9.30am-9pm,
Sun. 10am-2pm.

From June to September, hostesses wearing

MUSEUM OPENING TIMES

Museums generally open from 10am to 1/2pm and 4/4.30 to 7.30pm and close Sunday afternoons and Mondays (except for the Picasso Museum and the Tàpies and Miró Foundations). Opening times vary little in summer and winter, except at the Football Museum and the Olympic Gallery. Entry fees are around €3-6. Some galleries and museums offer a *combina do* ticket which allows entry to both and some offer a 'free day' (often the first Sunday of the month). It's also a good idea try to avoid the days when school parties get in free! Get a copy of *La Guia del Ocio*, a guide to exhibitions, concerts and shows, which gives up-to-date info and general opening times of historic buildings.

red and white uniforms and 'i' badges are assigned to strategic points and will be able to provide you with useful information.

The Barrio Gòtico:
in the shadow of history

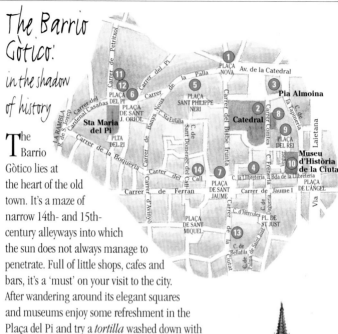

The Barrio Gòtico lies at the heart of the old town. It's a maze of narrow 14th- and 15th-century alleyways into which the sun does not always manage to penetrate. Full of little shops, cafes and bars, it's a 'must' on your visit to the city. After wandering around its elegant squares and museums enjoy some refreshment in the Plaça del Pi and try a *tortilla* washed down with *horchata* (barley drink).

❶ Plaça Nova★★

The ancient city of *Barcino*, whose name is carved in the square, was founded here. The remains of the 4th-century city walls contain two Roman towers flanking the del Bisbal Gate. One of them has a hollowed-out niche dedicated

to St Roch, the patron saint, whose feast-day is celebrated in full summer on 16th August. There is also an antiques market on Thursdays, Advent celebrations, and *sardana* dancing on Sundays. The 18th-century Baroque façade of the bishop's palace adds cachet to the setting. The same can't be said of the College of Architects built in 1961, though it does have a frieze by Picasso.

❷ Catedral★★★

Cathedral and terrace: open every day 10am–1pm, 5–7pm.
Museum: ☎ 93 310 25 80 (same opening times as cathedral).
Entry charge.

The magnificent Gothic façade actually dates from the 19th century. The cathedral is dedicated to St Eulàlia and was founded in the 13th century and completed in the 15th. It contains precious liturgical objects, such as the famous 16th-century *Christ of Lepanto* crucifix, said to have been on board the Spanish flagship of Don Juan of Austria at the time of the decisive victory against the Turks in 1571.

This medieval institution next to the cathedral was once an alms house providing a hundred poor people a day with a meal. Its subtle conversion to a Diocesan Museum is very successful, and is well worth climbing the few steps for.

❹ Catalonia Excursion Centre★★
Carrer del Paradis, 10
Open Tue.-Sat. 10am-2pm,
4-8pm, Sun. 10am-2pm.
Entry free.

You're treading on the remains of the Roman city here. A mill wheel embedded in the ground marks the entrance to the site. At the summit of *Mons Taber*, a temple dedicated to Augustus, built in the 1st century, was visible from far away. The columns you can see today were found at the start of the 20th century, while the bells of the nearby cathedral are a reminder that gods have been worshipped on this mound for thousands of years.

❺ Plaça de Sant Felip Neri and Shoe Museum★★
☎ 93 301 45 33
Open every day 11am-2pm,
closed Mon.
Entry charge.

REPARACIONS
AL
MOMENT

The baptismal fonts are said to have been used to christen the first six Indians brought back by Christopher Columbus in 1493. The delightful cloister is planted with orange-trees, magnolias, medlars and palm-trees. It's a cool oasis and a haven of peace that is sometimes broken by the cries of thirteen geese, their number symbolising Eulàlia's age at the time of her martyrdom.

❸ Pia Almoina and Diocesan Museum★★
Av. de la catedral, 4
☎ 93 315 22 13
Open Tue.-Sat.
10am-2pm,
5-8pm Sun.
11am-2pm.
Entry charge.

This shady little square often by-passed by visitors short of time occupies the site of a former cemetery. The Baroque façade of the church and two 16th-century houses form a harmonious group. The emblems of the Guilds of Shoemakers and Coppersmiths – the lion of St Mark and two spoons – are clearly visible. In the Shoe Museum, you can't miss the foot measuring 1.22m/4ft that was used as a model for the Christopher Columbus monument.

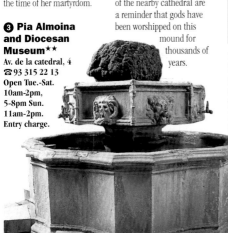

❻ Plaça del Pi and church★★★
Open every day 9am-1pm, 5-8.30pm.
Entry free.

The del Pi church is a perfect example of 14th-century Catalan Gothic. The square with its single pine-tree (*pi*) is delightful. In summer, sit on the terrace, sipping iced coffee to the sound of a saxophone. In winter, during Advent, the façades sparkle with a thousand lights. A slightly Bohemian air gives the place its charm.

❼ Plaça de Sant Jaume ★★
The institutional centre of the city that was once the site of the forum, the public square in Roman times. The name *Jaume* (James) comes from the church that stood here until 1824. Today the Town Hall (*Ajuntamient)* and Province of Catalonia (*Generalitat)* are in political opposition here. On feast days (Sant Jordi's and Sant Mercé's, see pp.14-17), the *castells* – pyramids of acrobats balancing precariously on top of one

another – defy the laws of gravity, while the three flags of Spain, Barcelona and Catalonia flutter in the breeze.

❽ Museu Frederic Marés★★★
Plaça St Iu, 5
☎ 93 310 58 00
Open Tue. & Thu. 10am-5pm, Wed., Fri. & Sat. 10am-7pm, Sun. 10am-2pm.
Entry charge.

In fine weather, pause on the patio, where tables and refreshments await you.

upstairs and see the collection of briar pipes, fob watches, pince-nez, parasols and fans.

❾ Plaça del Rei, Tinell and Chapel of St Agatha★★★
☎ 93 315 11 11
Open Jul. to Sep., Tue.-Sat. 10am-2pm, 4-8pm, Sun. 10am-2pm.
Entry charge.

This is the most remarkable group of buildings in the city. Climb the palace steps to reach the Saló del Tinell, the magnificent hall and throne room, built in the 14th century. It is here in this very room that the Catholic King Ferdinand and Queen Isabella, on a visit to Barcelona, received Columbus on his

The museum houses Spanish sculpture from the Middle Ages to the 19th century. If there are too many versions of *Virgin and Child* and *Descent from the Cross*, for your liking, go

return from the New World in 1493. On the walls, 13th-century frescoes illustrate this period of Catalan grandeur. The 14th-century palace chapel of

St Agatha is adorned with a renowned 15th-century painting, the *Constable's Altar-piece*, by Huguet. From the top of King Marti's turret you can see a maze of alleyways overlooked by a cluster of steeples.

⑩ Museu d'Història de la Ciutat★★
Combined entry ticket includes the Tinell.

This museum, dedicated to the history of the city, is housed in the beautiful 15th-century mansion, Casa Clariana-Padellas. You can see extensive Roman ruins discovered during work carried out in the 1930s and the remains of a Christian basilica.

⑪ La Granja Dulcinea★
Carrer Petritxol, 2
☎ 93 302 68 24
Open Mon.-Sun. 9am-1pm, 4.30-9pm.

A *granja* is a bit like a tearoom, where fresh farm produce takes pride of place. Highly recommended is the *suisso con ensaimada*, thick hot chocolate topped with whipped cream and accompanied by

tempting Majorcan cakes and pastries, all beneath the understanding eye of the old man in the photo pinned to the wall. Don't worry, everyone in Barcelona, young and old alike, indulge themselves here.

⑫ La Gavineteria Roca★★
Plaça del Pi, 3
☎ 93 302 12 41
Open Mon.-Fri. 8.45am-1.30pm, 4.15-8pm, Sat. 10am-2pm, 5-8pm.

Roca sells bladed instruments of all kinds. There's been a knife grinder here since 1911, specialising in cut-throat razors, manicure sets, scissors, knives and penknives. The *navaja de Albacete* with a curved handle will cost you 2,000 ptas. The extraordinary stainless-steel *Modernista* shop front, however, is not for sale.

⑬ Anormis★★
Carrer de la Ciutat, 3
☎ 93 302 30 04
Open Mon.-Fri. 9.30am-1pm, 4-8pm.

Entering this, one of the oldest shops in the old town, you may well come across the very cure you've been seeking for ages. Señor

⑭ THE *CALL*
The *Call* (alley) or ghetto conjures up one of the most flourishing facets of medieval Barcelona, the aljama, or Jewish community. Nowadays finding any trace of it requires a vivid imagination. The bloody pogrom of 1391 ended in fire and bloodshed. Now nothing remains but memories of the ambassadors, interpreters, financiers, astronomers, alchemists and eminent doctors who lived and worked here. Only Carreres del Call, Sant Ramon del Call and Sant Domènec del Call still bear witness to the past.

Anormis acts as herbalist, doctor, confidant and adviser to his customers and his formulae are only revealed in the strictest secrecy.

The Ribera:
past meets present

Living in the Ribera is like living in a village. Old crafts rub shoulders with fashionable institutions. The shop window of a humble upholsterer vies with the fashionable Galeria Maeght. Trendy designers work alongside glass-blowers, whilst the city's pensioners play cards and embroider. The streets are steeped in history, and are not only home to the church of Santa Maria del Mar, but also to the local tearooms and bookshops. One of the last fashionable quarters of the city, and not to be missed.

Pablo Picasso, Les Ménines.

of the most aristocratic streets in the city. The Palau is a fine example of the patrician structures of the late Middle Ages, inspired by northern Italy.

1 Palau de la Música★★★
C. de Sant Francesc de Paula, 2
☎ 93 295 72 00
Open Jun-Jul., Sep.-Oct. (closed Aug.).
Guided tour (charge) Mon.-Fri. 10am-3.30pm every 30 minutes (phone in advance).

Built in 1908 in the pure *Modernista* style by Domenech i Montaner, this concert hall has superb stained-glass windows, mosaics and sculpture, with an elaborate façade supported on three large columns. The accoustics are excellent, and it's worth asking at the box office to see if any reduced tickets are available on the night of a concert.

2 Museu Picasso★★★
Carrer Montcada, 15-19
☎ 93 319 63 10
Open Tue.-Sat. 10am-8pm, Sun. 10am-3pm.
Bookshop and restaurant. Entry charge.

Since 1963 the Palau Berenguer d'Aguilar has housed the works of Pablo Picasso. It opens onto one

The terracotta jars on the ground floor, used for storing oil, wine and water, show that the original inhabitants were

involved in trade. On the first floor, some of Picasso's youthful works evoke his brief, but intense encounter with Barcelona's Bohemian set. The room devoted to his interpretation of Velàsquez's famous painting *Las Meninas* is the highlight of a visit to the museum.

❸ Museu du Tèxtili i d'Indumentària★★
Carrer Montcada, 12
☎ **93 310 45 16**
Open Tue.-Sat. 10am-6pm, Sun. 10am-3pm.
Entry charge.

This museum, housed in the Palau de Los Marqueses De Lliό, is a Gothic masterpiece whose original structure has been preserved. You can sample some homemade pastries on the patio before seeing the collections. The Textile and Costume Museum traces the development of textiles over a period of 1,500 years, with precious Coptic cloth, Chantilly lace, embroidered damask, Indian calico, and creations by Worth and Balenciaga. Also on display are Catalan textile industry tools. Before leaving the palace, buy a few metres of fabric designed by Mariscal (€21.05 a metre/yard), the king of Barcelona design.

❹ Santa Maria del Mar★★★
Plaça Santa Maria
Open every day
9am-1.30pm, 4.30-8pm.

Situated on the waterfront, the church was originally called *Santa Maria de las Arenas* (of the sands). This early 14th-century Gothic building symbolises the prosperity of the merchants of the period. Many sail makers, stevedores and porters are buried in its walls. Built over half a century with remarkable unity of style, it has a wide nave and narrow aisles. In the Middle Ages Catalan sailors set sail for distant conquests to the cry of *Santa Maria*, their patron saint.

❺ Passeig del Born★★

The location for a market in medieval times, which sold goods from overseas including spices and medicines, it has a very grisly past. Heretics

condemned to death by the Spanish Inquisition were burned at the stake here. The Born was later turned into an open-air theatre and jousts (*bournar*), tournaments and other knightly celebrations took place. In 1874, the Merecat del Born was erected, a metal-structured market hall, nowadays used for temporary exhibitions.

❻ La Llotja★
Pla del Palau, 22
Open Mon.-Fri. 10.30am-1pm.

La Llotja market was a typically Mediterranean institution and very powerful. Originally, this market hall was open to the elements, but

in 1380 as business prospered and trade increased, a permanent building was erected. The *Consulat del Mar*, linked to the community of Catalan merchants overseas, was established here. Rebuilt in the 18th century, the low Gothic hall has been preserved and now houses the Stock Exchange and Academy of Fine Arts.

7 Pla de la Garsa★
Carrer Assaonadors, 13
☎ 93 315 24 13
Open Mon.-Sat. 1.15-5pm, 9pm-1am, Sun. 9pm-1am.

A short distance from the Picasso Museum, this wine bar has the charm of an old-fashioned bistrot. A broken tiled floor surrounds the bar made of *rajoles* (terracotta tiles) from Valencia. The wrought-iron spiral staircase is the pride of the owner, who'll recommend the *embotits i formatjes*, an excellent selection of cold ham and ewe's cheese washed down with a Rioja or Penedès wine (around €15).

8 Galeria Maeght★
Carrer Montcada, 25
☎ 93 310 42 45
Open Tue.-Sat. 10am-2pm, 4-8pm.

Aimé Maeght (1906-1981) opened this Barcelona temple to contemporary art in 1974.

Wassili Kandinsky at the Galeria Maeght.

Housed in the 15th-century Cervellò palace, it exhibits works by Kandinsky, Braque, Miró and Tàpies, as well as less well-known artists such

as Bennassar, Grau and Solano. You can purchase art books here, of course,

as well as graphic works by talented young artists and even special collector's editions.

9 La Casa Gispert★★★
Carrer Sombrerers, 23
☎ 93 319 75 35
Open Mon.-Fri. 9am-1.30pm, 4-7.30pm, Sat. 10am-2pm, 5-8pm.

Since 1851 the Gispert family have been *Mestres Torradors*, past masters in the art of coffee-roasting. From the gleaming black-and-gold shop front wafts the sweetish aroma of saffron, cinnamon and Ethiopian coffee. Sacks and jars overflow with dried fruits and spices as in an Oriental market. In the back shop, the old almond-grilling

oven is still going strong. A charming place and a delightful way to indulge the senses.

⑩ L'Euskal Etxea★
Placeta de Montcada, 1-3
☎ **93 310 21 85**
Open Tue.-Sun. morning 12.30-3.30pm, 9-11.30pm.

For *tapas* fans this restaurant offers a typical Basque selection including *txakas* (crab mayonnaise), *pimientos del piquillo* (green peppers) and mussel kebabs, accompanied by a local white *txacoli*, which are all the rage. This is a charming typically *Euskera* (Basque) restaurant, which also houses a cultural centre.

⑪ Ici et Là★★
Plaça Santa Maria del Mar, 2
☎ **93 268 11 67**
Open Mon. 4-8.30pm, Tue.-Sat. 10.30am-8.30pm.

A simple yet sophisticated shop opening onto a square cooled by the spray from a Gothic fountain. Small pieces of iron furniture,

multicoloured mosaic tables and ethnic objects mingle with the creations of young designers, which include brightly-coloured tablecloths

with contrasting traditional Catalan designs (a pair of tea towels costs €9.30).

⑬ REC CONTAL

The tanning and dyeing industries were set up on the banks of the stream that gave this street its name. The street names of the Ribera evoke the ancient crafts which were practised in them: *Assaonadors, Blanqueria, Corretger, Vidrieria, Corders, Carders, Argenteria, Flassaders* and *Esparteria* (tanning, tawing, welding, stained-glass window making, rope-making, carding, silversmithing, blanket-making and working with rushes). The shop-keeping mentality was born here and the Catalans have a nose for business.

⑫ Moska★★
Carrer dels Flassaders, 42A
☎ **93 310 17 01**
Open Tue.-Sat. 10am-5pm. Closed Mon. & Sun.

The name of this small boutique pays tribute to Calle Mosca, which meets at an angle with Calle Flassaders, famous for being the city's narrowest street. The owner of the shop sees her jewellery as a collection of small sculptures, and exhibits them as if they are on display in a museum.

The beautiful pieces are arranged in meticulously planned window displays designed by her architect husband. Here you'll find ancient pieces from Asia and Africa on sale alongside more contemporary works in such diverse materials as gold, silver, paper, resin, plastic and wood.

The Raval:
venture outside the old city walls

Better known as the Barrio Chino, the Raval has fascinated artists for a long time, with its pimps and prostitutes, transvestites, shady deals and more than a whiff of sleaze from the nearby port. Though for some years now cultural institutions have been moving in, adding a touch of respectability to the area. It's a cosmopolitan mix of locals and immigrants from Africa and Asia.

❶ Casa de la Caritat★★
Carrer de Montalegre, 5-7
☎ 93 306 41 00
Open Tue., Thu, Fri. 11am-2pm, 4-8pm, Wed. and Sat. 11am-8pm, Sun. 11am-7pm.
Entry charge.

A perfect example of the new living alongside the old. Built in 1714 on the site of a 14th-century convent, this former asylum and workhouse is now home to the Centre de Cultura Contemporania and is used for exhibitions of town planning. The superb patio (1714) and the façade (1993) harmonise well. At the back there is a lovely little café with a terrace.

❷ Museu d'Art Contemporáni★★★
Plaça dels Angels, 1
☎ 93 412 08 10
Open in summer: Mon., Wed., & Fri. 11am-8pm, Thu. & Sat. 11am-10pm, Sun. 10am-3pm. In winter: Mon., Wed., Thu. & Fri. 1-7.30pm, Sat. 10am-9pm, Sun. 10am-3pm.
Entry charge.

The museum was designed by the architect Richard Meier, very much a fan of whiteness and purity. This dazzling liner of a building is an absolute contrast to the nearby façades of the old buildings. Opened in 1995, it displays a good selection of work by mainly

Catalan and Spanish artists since 1945, though there is some foreign work too. Also known as MACBA for short.

3 Hospital de la Santa Creu★★
Carrer del Carme, 47-49/ Carrer de l'Hospital, 56 Patio open every day 10am-6pm.

Take a walk in the shade of the former 15th-century hospital garden, once a refuge for pilgrims in Catalonia. The vestibule of the Casa de Convalescencia is sumptuously decorated with ceramic scenes of the life of St Paul in green and yellow. Gaudí died here in 1926.

4 Sant Pau del Camp Monastery★★
Carrer de Sant Pau, 101 ☎ 93 441 00 01 Open Tue.-Sat. 7.30-8.45pm, Sun. 9.30am-1.30pm.

To escape the hustle and bustle of the street, step inside Sant Pau, the 12th-century Romanesque Benedictine monastery where you'll be struck by the tranquillity of the cloister. The parish priest will gladly give you an account of its history, if asked.

5 Palau Güell★
Carrer Nou de la Rambla, 3-5 ☎ 93 317 39 74 Open Mon.-Sat. 10am-2pm, 4-8pm. Entry charge.

This enigmatic palace was built in 1888 by Gaudí for his patrons, the Güell family. A tour of the building takes you through a turn-of-the-century interior with Gaudí's curved

BARRIO CHINO

The Barrio Chino, or Chinese quarter, owes its name to a report by the writer Francis Carcoi entitled 'China Town', yet you won't find a trace of Chinese immigration here. The district has been inhabited by Andalusians since the beginning of the 19th century. Immigrants from Pakistan and Africa arrived recently to join them, making the Barrio Chino a kind of Catalan melting-pot.

and twisting shapes, whilst the façade displays his supreme artistry in wrought-iron work. The architect's fervent nationalism is apparent in the form of an eagle holding the coat of arms of Catalonia.

6 El Indio★
Carrer Carme, 24 ☎ 93 317 54 42 Open Mon.-Sat. 10am-2pm, 4.30-8pm.

This is certainly one of the most attractive *Modernista* shop fronts in the city, but do go in and have a look round. The decor hasn't changed much for years with colourful remnants of cloth displayed on wooden racks and a patient cashier behind the till.

7 Pla dels Angels★★
Carrer de Ferlandina, 23 ☎ 93 443 31 03 Open every day 9am-midnight (closed Sun. pm and Tue. lunchtime).

During the summer months, this restaurant stretches as far as the museum square. It's popular with a young and trendy crowd and you can enjoy a pleasant meal at reasonable prices in a relaxed atmosphere.

The interior of Palau Güell.

The Ramblas:
a place to see and be seen

La Rambla lies at the heart of the city. The most famous street in Barcelona is lined with cafes, bars, shops, hotels and newspaper kiosks. It's always busy, no matter what hour of day, though evening is undoubtedly the liveliest time. In the morning little old ladies clutching string bags trot from the market to the Betlem church. In the evening three-card tricks, paintings and improvised acrobatics extract money from passers-by. The street cuts through the old town and the area is known as the Ramblas.

❶ Plaça de Catalunya★

This large and irregularly-shaped square is the link between the old town and 19th-century Eixample, and was first landscaped in 1854. It became the nerve centre of the city in 1925 with the building of the department store, El Corte Inglès, banks and hotels. Marks & Spencer now has a store here. On Sundays, you can buy *pipas* (sunflower seeds) to feed to the pigeons.

❷ Església de Betlem★★★
La Rambla, 107
Open every day 7.45am-9pm.
The façade of this church is a Baroque flight of fancy, with statues of St Ignacio de Loyola and St Francisco de Borja deep in conversation. Begun in 1681, it formed the nucleus of a complex of buildings occupied by the Jesuits until their expulsion in 1767. Sadly, the interior was gutted by fire during the Civil War in 1936. In the morning the low angle of the sun casts a theatrical light on one of the city's unique Baroque monuments.

❸ Palau de la Virreina★★★

La Rambla, 99
☎ 93 301 77 75
Open Tue.-Sat. 2-8pm,
Sun. 11am-3pm.
Entry charge.

Named after the Vice-reine of Peru, who lived here after the death of her husband, this is a graceful 18th-century addition to the district. It later became the site for exhibitions of the decorative arts. Take the main staircase to see the superb French-style decor.

❹ Mercat de la Boqueria★★★

La Rambla, 85-89
Open every day except Sun.
6am-9.30pm.

Stroll round this covered market which dates from 1860 and and enjoy the wonderful mediterranean feel. The locals chatter as they go round selecting the day's best buy and the stall holders call out to customers. The displays of fresh produce are really quite something to behold. If you wish to really blend in with the locals, stand at the *barra*, the bar, of the *Pinocho* kiosk and sample the Catalan-style tripe.

❺ Grand Teatre del Liceu★

La Rambla, 51-59
☎ 93 485 99 00
www.liceubarcelona.com
Tours: 9.45-11am.

The opera house, a symbol of 19th-century middle-class and industrial Barcelona, was built in 1844 and burnt down for the first time in 1861. It was rebuilt before suffering a bomb attack. It went up in flames again in 1994, but has just been restored. Fingers crossed this time.

❻ Hotel Oriente★

La Rambla, 45
☎ 93 302 25 58
Metro Drassanes.

This hotel was built on the site of the Franciscan College of St Bonaventura, of which only the old cloister was preserved. In its heyday notable people such as Hemingway stayed here, as well as various Hollywood stars and toreadors. In the 19th century it was still one of the biggest hotels in Europe and in 1975 Antonioni filmed *The Passenger* here with Jack Nicholson.

❼ Plaça Reial★★

Under the 19th-century arcades it's a fascinating mix of cafes selling *calamares a la romana* (squid), dealers selling '*chocolate*' or hashish, stamp dealers at the Sunday-morning market, palmists,

artists and tramps, with the odd policeman keeping a watchful eye. The terrace of the **Quinze Nits** (see p. 79) is a good place from which to watch the proceedings. Watch out for the street lights which are the work of a youthful Gaudí.

❽ Santa Monica Art Centre★
La Rambla, 7
☎ 93 412 22 79
Open Mon.-Sat. 11am-2pm, 5-8pm, Sun. 11am-3pm
Entry charge.

In 1988 Pinon and Viaplana converted this former 17th-century convent into a contemporary art centre, more or less successfully marrying two styles of architecture. Happily they managed to preserve the old cloister. The bookshop is well stocked in books on design.

❾ Boadas★
Carrer Tallers, 1
☎ 93 318 88 26
Open Mon.-Sat. noon-2pm.

This copper and mahogany bar on the corner of the Ramblas is often frequented by politicians and intellectuals. It is reputed to have mixed the best cocktails in the city,

mojitos, margaritas and dry martinis, since 1933. The founder, Boadas, learnt the secrets of his trade in Havana, and the barman is of course a real expert.

❿ Casa Beethoven★★
La Rambla, 97
☎ 93 301 48 26
Open Mon.-Fri. 9am-8pm, Sat. 9am-1.30pm, 5-8pm.

Appropriately enough for its name, the owner is a pianist. The wooden shelves and the counter give off the sweetish smell of resin. For nearly a century they have been selling sheet music, catering for all genres from traditional *sardanas* to bossa nova, samba, rumba, Schubert and, of course, De Falla.

⓫ Xancò★
La Rambla, 78-80
☎ 93 318 09 89
Open Mon.-Fri. 10am-2pm, 4.30-8.30pm, Sat. 10am-2pm, 5-8.30pm.

Time has stood still at Xancò. Made-to-measure shirts have

been produced here since 1820, adapting to changing fashions as the years have passed and all carefully arranged on carved wooden shelves. You can have your initials embroidered on the shirts and can choose from twenty-nine colours in a fine cotton poplin from around €60. The counter alone is worth the visit and you'll be able to see the superb oriental shop sign opposite B. Cuadros at no. 82.

⓬ Café de l'Òpera★
La Rambla, 74
☎ 93 302 41 80
Open Mon.-Thu. 9am-2.30pm, Fri. & Sat. 9am-3pm.

This bar opposite the Liceu theatre was established in 1929 on the premises of a former chocolate shop, La Mallorquina, and is open and smoke-filled at all hours. The Thonet chairs and tarnished mirrors lend it a distinctive atmosphere. In the 1960s, it saw gatherings of Latin-American novelists, whose work was avidly consumed

by the city. *Tertulias*, lengthy discussions on any topic from jazz to alternative medicine, were constantly in full swing. Nowadays, however, the bar is mainly frequented by tourists.

⓭ Herbolari Farran★★
Plaça Reial, 18
☎ **93 304 20 05**
Open Mon.-Sat. 9.30am-2pm, 4.30-8pm.

Go along pretty Bacardi passage to this first-rate herbalist's. The fragrant plants and herbs exude health and well-being. You'll find herbal teas to heal all ills, fragrant essences and a surprisingly wide choice of so-called miracle cures.

⓮ Antiga Casa Figueras★★
La Rambla, 83
☎ **93 301 60 27**
Open Mon.-Sun. 8.30am-9pm.

The house of Escribà, heirs to a family of famous Catalan confectioners, has celebrated its 90th anniversary and still smells as good as ever since the truffles and bars of bitter chocolate are made on the premises. Don't miss the *pastas alimenticias* shop sign and the extraordinary *Modernista* decor –

sculpture, mosaics and stained-glass windows, all the applied arts on display here celebrate the art of good food.

'Rambla' comes from the Arab word *ramla*, meaning sand. La Rambla follows the course of what was once a river. Until the 14th century it served as the western boundary of the city and marks the site of a 13th-century rampart, which allowed access to the city via the Santa Anna, Porta-ferissa, Boqueria and Drassana gates. Lamp-posts at six junctions along the *passeig* mark their former position. A mosaic of *azulejos* at the start of Portaferissa street, shows the layout of the old walls.

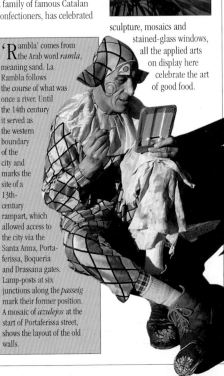

L'Eixample: the marvels of Modernisme

At the turn of the century the Eixample, literally 'the extension', became the most prestigious part of the city. Many of its *Modernista* buildings house exclusive shops. The trendy lay siege to *Vinçon* to acquire the latest designer lamps, whilst swarms of eager tourists descend on *Loewe* and re-emerge triumphant, brandishing designer leather goods. Meanwhile, seated on benches in the wide avenues outside, businessmen pore over their their newspapers, one of the morning's ritual pleasures. It's an affluent and busy district, full of opulence.

① Passeig de Gràcia★

From 1890 to 1925, Passeig de Gràcia was an upper-middle class residential area. The city's first gas lamps were installed here and it became a fashionable place to walk at turn of the last century. The bourgoisie paraded in their horse-drawn carriages, their children accompanied by Galician nannies. Carnivals alternated with military processions, so there was frequently a festive air.

② Museu de la Música★★★

Avinguda Diagonal, 373
☎ **93 416 11 57**
Open Tue.-Sun. 10am-2pm, Wed. 1-8pm.
Entry charge.

Known as the Palau Quadras, this building was erected by the architect Puig i Cadafalch in 1906. The beautiful staircase and mosaic floor, columns with floral capitals and stone fountain of the entrance hall all add up to a building of great harmony.

The collection of musical instruments from the 16th to 20th century is particularly rich in guitars and they have an impressive display of organs.

❸ Casa Milà★★
Carrer Provença, 261-265
☎ 93 484 59 00
Rooms open Mon.-Sun.
10am-8pm.
Entry charge.

Gaudí's last, astonishing secular building was built between 1905 and 1910. Known locally as la Pedrera (the quarry), its undulating limestone façade – more sculpture than architecture – was to culminate in a tribute to the Virgin Mary, but his patrons, the Milà family, objected. Gaudí abandoned the project in order to devote his time and energy to La Sagrada Familia (see p. 31). Casa Milà houses an attic exhibition space, a reconstruction of a *Modernista* flat, a gift and bookshop and, of course, the fabulous roof terrace with its strangely curving chimneys.

❹ Manzana de la Discordia★★★
Casa Lleó Morera,
Casa Batlló, Casa Amatller,
Passeig de Gràcia
☎ 93 496 12 45
No tours.

At the turn of the century each of the great families

commissioned the most celebrated of the city's architects to erect suitably grand buildings in order to etch their names in posterity. The clashing styles of these buildings designed between 1898 and 1906, resulted in the name Manzana de la Discordia, or 'Block of Discord'. Architectural styles pre-dating the industrial revolution were used as well as the *Modernista* style (see p. 22). These lavish residences were designed and built on a strict rectangular grid plan, like pieces on a chess board, as you can see on the map.

❺ Casa Calvet★★
Carrer de Casp, 48
No tours.

This was Gaudí's first building, and the only one for which he was awarded a prize in 1900. There are several strange things about it, including the three saints' heads provocatively watching passers-by, richly-decorated pulley supports and wrought-iron balustrade projections which soften and round off the rough stonework façade.

❻ Fundació Antoni Tàpies★★★
Carrer d'Aragò, 255
☎ 93 487 03 15
Open Tue.-Sun. 10am-8pm.
Entry charge.

This insitution is the result of the combined genius of two famous Catalan artists. In 1886 the architect Domenech i Montaner designed the Montaner i Simon publishing house, which later became the Antoni Tàpies Foundation. The cast iron and glass open-work exterior is ideal for exhibiting Tàpies' works (see p. 29). The building also houses a library and temporary exhibitions.

Tinçon (a play on words meaning 'I'm sleepy') is the little sister of the trendy shop Vinçon (see below) and sells everything you could think of to do with slumber, including sheets, pillowcases, bed linen and even books on the subject. It also boasts the traditional high quality and innovative design found at its big sister, Vinçon.

everything here from the most avantgarde furniture to the latest gadgets for the bathroom, kitchen and office. The superb window displays have also become a showroom of its contemporary (and future) design.

7 Universitat★
Gran Via de les Corts Catalanes, 585
No tours.

The first university of Catalonia was founded at Lerida in 1300. At the start of the 15th century, King Martín the Humane introduced formalised teaching in the arts and medicine. The university had to move to Cervera in the 18th century, but the present neo-Romanesque building by Elies Rogent, with an attractive courtyard and gardens, was not built until 1861. The library contains more than two million volumes, manuscripts and priceless early printed books.

8 Tinçon★★
Carrer de Rosselló, 246
☎ 93 215 60 50
www.vincon.com
Open Mon.-Sat. 10am-2pm, 4.30-8.30pm.

9 Vinçon★★
Passeig de Gràcia, 96
☎ 93 215 60 50
www.vincon.com
Open Mon.-Sat. 10am-2pm, 4.30-8.30pm.

One day, a German by the name of Vinçon, decided to make his name in contemporary design. It was a wise decision as nowadays his shop stocks the best and most complete selection of design items for the home. You'll find

10 Tragaluz ★
Passatge de la Concepció, 5
☎ 93 487 06 21
Open every day
1.30-4pm, 8.30pm-1am.

This very fashionable restaurant is a perfect example of its kind. The refined surroundings and quiet atmosphere offer a choice of stylish nouvelle

cuisine dishes to match the setting, a turn-of-the-century villa with a very sophisticated designer decor. Choose a mezzanine table for the best view (around €24).

⑪ Antonio Miró★★
Carrer del Consell de Cent, 349
☎ 93 487 06 70
Open Mon.-Sat. 10am-8.30pm (closed in winter 12.30-4.30pm).

⑫ Le Café du Centre★★★
Carrer Girona, 69
☎ 93 488 11 01
Open Mon.-Fri. 7am-3am, Sat. 7.30pm-3am; in Feb. 10am-12.30pm, 4.30-8.30pm.

During the Republic (1931-1936), Le Café du Centre was a very reputable and distinguished

The Barcelona designer Antonio Miró is well-regarded all over the world. The warm and graphic decor of his shop was designed by Pilar Lìbano in keeping with Miró's elegant line of clothes for both men and women. Women's suits cost from €420.

gaming house. When gambling was prohibited, it was converted into a *bodega*, a wine bar serving a selection of cold ham and sausages, *embotits*, and *pa amb tomàquet*, slices of toasted bread with olive oil and tomatoes (€12). Ask for a table where *L'Avi*, a legendary croupier, shuffled the cards and established his reputation.

⑬ Roca Jewellers★★
Passeig de Gràcia, 18
☎ 93 318 32 66
Open Mon.-Fri. 9.30am-1.30pm, 4.30-8pm, Sat. (in winter only) 10am-1.30pm, 5-8pm.

The interior of this jeweller's shop, the work of the architect Josep Lluis Sert, a friend of Joan Miró, is a superb example of rationalist architecture. Space, light and colour combine with the furniture to lend the decor great purity. It's the perfect setting for a jewellers and is definitely worth a visit.

THE CERDÀ PLAN

When the ramparts disappeared in 1854 Idelfons Cerdà was given the task of drawing up plans for the Eixample. Belonging to the generation of Proudhon, Hegel and the Romantic Movement he planned a modern, democratic city based on a grid shape cut diagonally by avenues. Work began in 1859 and an elegant and airy new district was born, with residential and apartment blocks, gardens and wide avenues.

Ciutadella: a green haven

The Ciutadella park looks inviting enough for a stroll, and in summer provides an escape from the mugginess of the city. Lovers kiss on the boating lake while laughing children chase pigeons along the paths, try out their bikes and greet *Copito de Nieve*, the albino gorilla and zoo mascot.

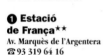

It's an open space filled with light that brightens up the dark, cramped maze of the old districts.

❶ Estació de França★★
Av. Marquès de l'Argentera
☎ 93 319 64 16
Open every day 6am-11.30pm.

The Estació de França station was built for the 1929 Universal Exhibition by the engineer A. Montaner, and

restored in 1992. It was one of the most modern stations of its time, with metal arches spanning over 30m/100ft overhanging the platforms. Its splendid architecture can still produce gasps even today.

❷ Parc de la Ciutadella★
Three entrances: Pg. Picasso, Pg. Pujades, C. Wellington.
Open every day 10am-5pm in winter, 9.30am-7.30pm in summer.

On 11 September 1714, the city surrendered to its new king, Philip V of Spain. A section of the Ribera district was razed to the ground (see p. 40) in order to build a stronghold, symbolic of the subjugation of Barcelona by the Bourbons. The fortress was attacked in the 19th century during a resurgence

of Catalan nationalism. It was demolished in 1868 and the area converted into a park.

❸ Parc Zoològic★

Parc de la Ciutadella
☎ 93 225 67 80
Open every day 10am-5pm
in winter, 9.30am-7.30pm in
summer.
Entry charge.

The Parc Zoològic occupies a good portion of the south-east part of the park. Colourful birds from all over the world, toucans, macaws and parrots, marmosets, dolphins, are all housed here, but the star exhibit is *Copito de Nieve* (Snowflake), the unique albino gorilla.

❹ Museu d'Art Modern de Catalunya★★★

Parc de la Ciutadella
☎ 93 319 57 28
Open every day except Mon.
10am-7pm Sun. 10am-
2.30pm.
Entry charge.

Housed in the former arsenal, the museum presents a marvellous insight into turn-of-the-century Barcelona. The collections cover the period from 1830 to 1930. Look out for Fortuny, Russinyol, Casas, Mir and Nonell. If you're

a fan of *Modernista* and Noucentista architecture (see p. 22), visit the room dedicated to the decorative arts, which reflects the interior decoration of the buildings. Gaspar Homar's precious marquetry and the rippling lines of Gaudí chairs will delight the eye.

❺ Parc de la Ciutadella Umbracle and Hivernacle★★

☎ 93 295 40 17
Café Hivernacle open
Mon.-Fri. 10am-midnight,
Sat.-Sun. 10am-5pm.

This is an English-style park with two large glass-houses. One was called the Umbracle, built in 1883, a combination of ironwork columns and beams. It once housed a botanical school, but now contains teak deck chairs where you can lounge and dream of the tropics. The other, the Hivernacle, has a light ironwork structure, perfect for relaxing on a balmy summer evening.

❻ Arc de Triomf and Museu de Zoologia★★

Passeig Picasso
☎ 93 319 69 12
Open Tue.-Sun. 10am-2pm,
Thu. 10am-6.30pm.
Entry charge.

The Parc de la Ciutadella staged the Universal Exhibition of 1888. The Arc de Triompf was erected as a monumental entrance, opening onto the Passeig San Joan. The former restaurant of the Exhibition now houses the Museu de Zoologia, which contains displays of stuffed animals and birds. Designed by Domenech i Montaner, the *Castell dels Tres Dragons* (Castle of the Three Dragons), as it came to be known, has medieval and Moorish elements.

❼ SET PORTES RESTAURANT★★

Passeig Isabel II, 14
☎ 93 319 30 33.
Open every day 1pm-1am.

An institution and cult venue with a visitors' book that has Che Guevara's signature alongside those of Manolete, John Wayne, Garcia Lorca, Miró and Ava Gardner. The 19th-century beams lit by rustic lamps are the ideal setting for a *paella marinera* or black rice from the Empordà (around €18).

C. de Portal · Sta Madrona · R. de Sta Mónica · LA RAMBLA · Av. de les Drassanes

Carrer

Museu Marítim ②

PLAÇA PORTAL DE LA PAU ①

Passeig   Moll   de   la

Moll de Bosch y Alsina

C. d'En Gignas · Ample · C. de la Fusteria · Via Laietána

La Mercè

PL. DE LA MERCÈ · Carrer · de · la · Mercè ④ ⑤

Colom Fusta ⑤

PLAÇA D'ANTONI LÓPEZ ⑦

Moll de les Drassanes ③ · Rambla de Mar

Las Golondrinas

Moll d'Espanya ⑥

The port: the call of the sea

The ideal way to approach Barcelona is by boat, as people did in the 19th century. Barcelona's wealth comes from the sea. Until 1900 visitors to Barcelona landed by rowing boat. Nowadays, if you feel like seeing the port, you need to cross the elegant Rambla de Mar footbridge to the Moll d'Espanya, a recent addition to the city. On Sundays, families come here to relax, proud to be part of this new capital of the Mediterranean which has, once more, resumed its vocation.

❶ Christopher Columbus Monument★

Plaça Portal de la Pau
☎ 93 302 52 24
Open 25 Sep.-30 Mar. Mon.-Fri. 10am-1.30pm, 3.30-6.30pm, Sat.-Sun. 10am-6.30pm; 1 Apr.-31 May, Mon.-Fri. 10am-2pm, 3.30-7.30pm, Sat.-Sun. 10am-7.30pm; 1 Jun.-24 Sep. every day 9am-8.30pm. Entry charge.

The 50m/165ft high column was erected for the Universal Exhibition of 1888, in homage to Christopher Columbus. From the top, you can pay your respects to the Genoese (or

Catalan, as they say here) explorer at close range. His finger isn't pointing in the direction of America, but towards the Mediterranean, the source of the city's wealth.

❷ Drassanes and Museu Marítim★★

Avinguda Drassanes
☎ 93 301 18 71
Open Mon.-Sun. 10am-7pm Entry charge.

In terms of size, the ships built here from the 14th to 17th centuries were unique in Europe. The industrial activity of the Drassanes, the medieval

shipyards, was prolific. Numerous vessels were launched, from commercial ships to warships. At the Museu Marítim, you can discover more about this industry, admire the replica of the Royal galley that took part in the Battle of Lepanto (1571) and even set out on 'The Great Sea Adventure' without fear of sea spray, since it's a special film show.

❸ Las Golondrinas, la Rambla de Mar★

Porta de la Pau
☎ 93 442 31 06
Departures every 35 minutes Mar.-Oct. every day 11am-8pm; Nov.-Feb. Sat.-Sun. 11am-4pm and weekday mornings. Boarding charge.

To explore the port at water level, board a *golondrina*, a small boat moored at the quay. You'll be told the history of the harbour, whose first stone was laid in the 15th century. Since 1994, la Rambla de Mar, a swing footbridge in the form of a magnificent metal wave, has been outlined against the sky. It was designed by Viaplana and Pinon.

pirates. The Virgin of La Mercè, the city's highly venerated patron saint, is celebrated on 22 and 24 September, with fireworks, parades of giants and *castellers* (see p. 16).

❺ Carrer de la Mercè and Moll de la Fusta★

Looking for a street with some *tapas*? There's **Pulperia** at 16 Carrer de la Mercè, with *patatas bravas* (a potato dish) and fried octopus to whet your appetite.

❹ Church of La Mercè and Carrer Ample★

Plaça de la Mercé
Open Mon.-Sat. 10am-1pm, 6-8.30pm, Sun. 10am-1.30pm, 7-8.30pm.

In the 18th century this district saw the building of the aristocratic residences on Carrer Ample. You'll have the best view of the Baroque façade of the basilica from the square with its imposing statue of Neptune. The Church gained a reputation for buying back Catalan prisoners from the Barbary

❼ CERVANTÈS' HOUSE★★★

Passeig Colom, 2
No tours.

According to local tradition, no. 2 is nicknamed *Casa Cervantès*. Apparently the writer stayed here during a visit in 1610. The stone façade of the house can be distinguished by its ornate windows. Perhaps behind one of them Cervantès imagined *Don Quijote* on the beach of Barceloneta, fighting the White Moon knight.

Bodega la Plata at no. 28. serves local white wine from a *porrò* (see p. 11), accompanied by grilled sardines, which are a real 'must'. If you prefer more trendy places, try the **Moll de la Fusta**. In the 1980s the docks were demolished to create this promenade lined with bars and restaurants. One of the high notes is the sculpture by Roy Lichtenstein (1992), *la Cara de Barcelona* (the face of Barcelona), a colourful creation that stands out against the blue sky.

❻ Le Moll d'Espanya★★

Maremagnum shopping centre:
Open every day 11am-11pm.
Aquarium:
☎ 93 221 74 74
Open every day 9.30am-11pm (9pm in winter)
Entry charge.
Imax: ☎ 93 225 11 11
Entry charge.

This is the new place to go if you're interested in the natural world. You can walk through the aquarium's 80m/260ft transparent tunnel and watch the dozen or so sharks at play, find out about the life of the beaver from the Imax cinema's 360° screen, buy 'organic' cotton shirts from Peru at Natura and a toy for the children at Imaginarium (see p. 93). And finally, you can treat yourself to a delicious vegetarian lunch.

From Barceloneta to Port Olímpic: an up-to-date coastline

Since 1992, the slogan *Barcelona oberta al mar* (Barcelona open to the sea) has become a fashionable theme. Town planners have transformed the coastline. Once you dined with your feet practically in the water in the *chiringuitos*, old family eateries that were abruptly torn down. If you're nostalgic for some Barceloneta 'local colour' then head for its central streets. You'll see washing fluttering on balconies, old people out for a breath of fresh air in their slippers, and cafés echoing to cheers as Barça score another goal.

been given a facelift, but remains a fine example of industrial architecture. These 'general warehouses for trade and commerce' house the new Museum of Catalan History,

❶ Marina Port Vell★★

The city hasn't always benefited from the sheltered port it has today. Until the 19th century ships had to stay out at sea while small craft transferred their merchandise to the shore. Port Vell is the old port, whose main feature today is the Maremagnum leisure complex of shops and bars. The marina is a recent addition (1992), and the yachts now add a touch of luxury to one of the oldest industrial parts of the port.

❷ Palau de Mar, Museu d'Història Catalunya★★★
Plaça Pau Vila
☎ 93 225 47 00
Open Tue., Thu., Fri., Sat. 10am-7pm (8pm the docks). Entry charge.

The Palau de Mar, part of the 19th-century docks, is an old warehouse which has recently spread over two floors. Great moments in Catalan history are presented in an educational and entertaining way, through creative displays, films, special effects, interactive screens and hands-on exhibits. Afterwards, you can enjoy something to eat on the terrace of the docks and dream of pirates and buccaneers.

❸ Moll dels Pescadors★★
Cable car open every day 11am-7pm (in good weather).
Entry charge.

The fishermen's jetty is only accessible during the fish auctions, when the place becomes a hive of activity from daybreak onwards as the fish wholesalers bid for the best parts of the catch. At night the

jetty is lit by the glow from the light of the old beacon (1772). St Sebastiàn's Tower is a familiar sight in the port and forms the terminus for the cable-car, which you can take back to Monjuïc.

❹ Barceloneta and its beach★★
Barceloneta is home to part of the city's folklore. It was

created in the 18th century, when the Ribera (see p. 40) was razed to the ground to build the Ciutadella (see p. 54). Its inhabitants had to wait until 1753 to be re-housed in Barceloneta. It has retained the charm of some of the old Mediterranean cities – you could easily be in Palermo or Naples. The people of Barcelona bathed at the Banos

St Sebastiàn and the Banos Orientales at the turn of the last century. Today, however, there's a five-kilometre stretch of palm-fringed beach popular with bathers and sun-worshippers alike.

❺ Church of St Miquel del Port★
Open every day 7am-1.45pm, 4.30-8pm.

This church was built when Barceloneta was in its infancy, in 1753, in honour of St Miquel, Barceloneta's

patron saint. Its façade is a fine example of Baroque architecture. In summer, it's delightfully cool and children play football outside in the square to cries of 'Força Barça'.

❻ Passeig Marítim, water tower and gasometer★
Passeig Marítim links 18th-century Barceloneta with the new Port Olímpic. As you walk along, you'll discover what remains of the area's industrial past. The *Modernista* silhouette of the water tower by J.Domenech i Estapà, built in 1906, is very striking and the old metal structure of the former gasometer will soon become the centrepiece of a park.

❼ Port Olímpic and Whale by Frank Gehry★★

The designer restaurants of Port Olímpic have replaced the cheaper, unassuming restaurants which lined the shore just a few years ago. It's quite usual to see several

❽ Arts Hotel★
Carrer de la Marina 19-21
☎ **93 221 10 00.**

Two towers dominate Port Olímpic. One of them, designed by Ortiz i Leon, houses Mapfre Insurance, the second is the luxurious Arts-Ritz-Carlton hotel. Its Terraza

the future – the Olympic Village, where athletes were housed during the 1992 Olympic Games. Manuel Vázquez Montalbán, the writer, wrote: *'The new Olympic Village is like an Oxford graduate playing cricket at the doors of the Bronx'.*

generations gather round a table for a family meal on Sunday. Grab an ice-cream or some *pipas* (roasted sunflower seeds) and take a stroll along the quays in the afternoon. A vast bronze whale is 'beached' here. Its 50m/165ft skeleton was designed by the architect Frank Gehry. In 1992 during the Barcelona Olympic Games, the watersport events were started from here.

bar (open every day 7am-2am) has one of the best views of Frank Gehry's whale, not to mention an overview of the port itself. The hotel's choice of *puros* (cigars) and *cavas* (local champagne) cocktails is quite unique. For 'designer *tapas*' try **Goyescas**, the hotel restaurant (open Mon.-Fri. 1-10pm, Sat. evenings only, closed Sun.).

❾ Nova Icària★
Nova Icària is the latest redevelopment project for 130 hectares/320 acres of coastline. It has appropriated part of the Poble Nou, the 'Catalan Manchester' of the 19th century, where only a few factory chimneys remain as a reminder of the area's industrial past. In the 1990s, architects backed by property developers, created the city of

❿ Baja Beach Club★★★
Passeig Marítim
☎ **93 225 91 00**
Summer: open every day 1pm-5am.

Winter: open Thu.-Sun. 1pm-5am.

One of the most recent of the new bars which go in and out of fashion so quickly, the Beach Club is the latest trendy venue, a disco, café and

restaurant all rolled into one. It features rather vulgar shows and sexy waitresses, so consider yourself warned! The menu is American-style, but people really come here more for the entertainment than for the food.

⑪ Two open-air sculptures★★★

The streets and squares of Barcelona include over 430 monuments. Many of them were erected during the first thirty years of the 20th century, but their number

multiplied in the 1980s and 1990s. One example from what you might term this open-air museum is Antoni Llena's *David and Goliath* (1993). Another is by Rebecca Horn. Her sculpture *Hommage to Barceloneta*

(1992) is to be found on the beach. It evokes the *chiringuitos*, the little kiosks selling food which have since vanished.

⑫ L'Antiga Casa Solé★★

Carrer Sant Carlos, 4
☎ **93 221 50 12**
Open Tue.-Sun. 1-4pm, 8.30-11pm.

This port bistrot, which opened in 1903, still has four of its original marble tables. Its waiters still wear white jackets and the beer is still draught. The open-plan kitchen is clearly visible to the diners who can see the delicious

dishes being prepared in front of them (see p. 10). *Sarsuela* (Catalan fish stew) was invented here and Casa Solé has been serving delicious traditional dishes ever since.

> ### *LOS CHIRINGUITOS*
>
> From 1941 onwards, fishermen's families traditionally prepared simple meals and snacks for bathers on the beach at Barceloneta, cooked in *chiringuitos*, little kiosks. These kiosks proliferated in the San Sebastiàn and Los Orientales areas, and were only open in summer. However, in 1991, the kiosks were sadly demolished, and part of the city's folklore and history disappeared along with them.

Diagonal Pedralbes: the city heights

M ountains and plains, sky and sea, Pyrenees and Mediterranean, this duality defines the Catalan country and its capital. For centuries the lure of a vista across the countryside or over the sea has drawn the people of Barcelona to its heights. Monasteries, villas, gardens and parks are dotted around the hillsides. In summer the light breezes are heaven-sent and open-air cafes are much in demand.

❶ Jardíns and Palau de Pedralbes★★

Avinguda Diagonal, 686
Museu de les Arts Decoratives
☎ 93 280 50 24
Museu de Ceràmica
☎ 93 280 16 21
Open Tue.-Sat. 10am-6pm, Sun. 10am-3pm.
Joint ticket.

This royal residence was built in the 1920s on land that once belonged to Don Güell. It houses the Museu de les Arts Decoratives and Museu de Ceràmica. There are unique pieces with enamel decoration by Artigas, Miró and Picasso.

❷ Monestir de Pedralbes★★

Baixada Monestir, 9
☎ 93 203 92 82
Open Tue.-Sun. 10am-2pm.
Entry charge.

One of the most attractive places to take a walk in the city. The name Pedralbes probably comes from the Latin *petras albas* (white stone). Commissioned around 650 years ago by Elisende de Montcada, wife of Jaume II, the church was consecrated in 1327. On her husband's death the queen retreated to the monastery surrounded by her

court. The three-storey cloisters evoke some 600 years of convent life, and are a fine illustration of Catalan Gothic architecture. In St Michael's chapel, the murals of Ferrer Bassa are evidence of the close ties between the Italians and Catalans in the 14th century.

❸ Thyssen-Bornemisza Collection★★★

Baixada Monestir, 9
☎ 93 280 14 34
Open Tue.-Sun. 10am-2pm.
Entry charge.

Since 1993, the Monastery of Pedralbes has exhibited part of the Thyssen-Bornemisza art Collection. Former dormitories of the St Clare of Assisi order of nuns were converted to house the collection, more evidence of the close links between medieval Italy and Catalonia.

It features 13th to 18th-century paintings from European Schools. If you're short of time, the highlights are Fra Angelico's *Virgin of Humility*, Titian's *Virgin and Child*, Tintoretto's *Portrait of the Senator*, Ruysdaël's *Seascape*, Canaletto's *Bucentaure* and Guardi's *St Mark's Square*.

❹ Entrance to the Finca Güell★★

Avinguda Pedralbes, 7.

The main gate and entrance pavilions of the Finca Güell by Gaudí once again demonstrate his tireless ornamental inventiveness. The Moorish caretaker's lodge could be mistaken for a sultan's harem, and the dragon standing guard is undoubtedly a Catalan Art Nouveau wrought-iron masterpiece, with menacing jaws ready to discourage any unwanted visitors. But don't let it put you off!

❺ Avinguda Diagonal★

This avenue crosses the city from east to west and was planned in 1859, like

L'Eixample (see p. 50). At the top of the avenue is the business centre, with luxury hotels, insurance companies, large department stores (Illa and Corte Inglès, see p. 94) and banks. The façade of the Caixa de Pensions displays a logo designed by Miró. This 5-pointed star is the emblem of one of the most powerful banking organisations in Europe. Avinguda Diagonal is now being extended to the sea.

❻ THE ASCENT OF THE TIBIDABO★★★

If you'd like to see some views, take a taxi to the foot of the Tibidabo (10 minutes from Pedralbes). Then take the *tramvía blau*, one of the last vestiges of Barcelona's tram system. This 'electric' ascent to the summit gives you the opportunity to admire the *Modernista* villas built by the Barcelona middle classes at the turn of the century. Every respectable family had a *torre* (villa) in the countryside. At the end of the journey, take a rest on the terrace of the **Venta**, a quaint Moorish open-air café.

Montjuïc: the reclaimed hill

Montjuïc was named after the Jewish community that once lived here. Given a costly facelift for the 1992 Olympic Games, the people of Barcelona now mainly come for the fresh air, though there's a lot to do and see. You can have a picnic, stroll along the terraces of the Miró Foundation, place a bet at the Plaça d'Espanya greyhound track, or, if you really must, go for a jog – the marathon entrance to the Olympic stadium isn't far away.

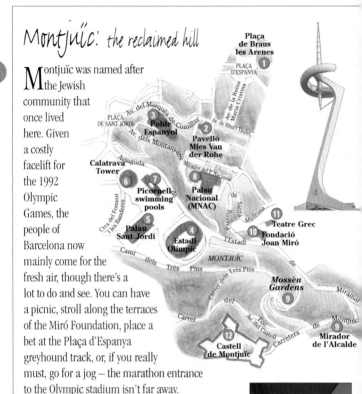

Plaça de Braus les Arenes **①**
PLAÇA D'ESPANYA
Av. del Marquès de Comillas
Av. de la Reina María Cristina
Av. de Rius I Taulet
PLAÇA DE SANT JORDI
③ Poble Espanyol
② Pavelló Mies Van der Rohe
Av. dels Montanyans
Avinguda
Calatrava Tower **⑥**
Ctra del Foment i les Banderes
Mirador del P. Nacional
⑦ Picornell swimming pools
⑧ Palau Nacional (MNAC)
Santa Madrona
⑤ Palau Sant Jordi
④ Estadi Olímpic
l'Estadi
⑪ Teatre Grec
⑩ Fondació Joan Miró
Camí dels Tres Pins
MONTJUÏC
Carrer dels Tres Pins
Mossèn Gardens **⑨**
Miramar
del
Carrer
Foc
Av. del Castell
Carretera
de Montjuïc
Mirador de l'Alcalde **⑨**
⑫ Castell de Montjuïc

❶ Carrer de Llancà and Plaça de Braus les Arenes ★★
Open Mon., Fri., Sat., Sun. 11am-2pm, 5-9pm, Tue. Wed. and Thu. 5-9pm
Free entry.

The Plaça d'Espanya, at the site of a former crossroads, was built for the 1929 Universal Exhibition (see p. 67). At its centre is an ornate fountain by J.M. Jujol, a colleague of Gaudí, which represents the rivers of the Iberian Peninsula. To the north lies the 'neo-Moorish' bull-ring of 1899 which is no longer in use as the Catalans despise the bull-fighting lifestyle of Madrid.

❷ Pavelló Mies Van der Rohe ★★
Av. del Marquès de Comillas
☎ 93 423 40 16
Open every day 10am-8pm.
Entry charge.

The Pavelló d'Alemanya lies at the foot of the Montjuïc. It was destroyed at the end of the 1929 Universal Exhibition, but then was reconstructed in 1986. It has a simple, abstract shape, made of marble, stone, onyx and glass.

❸ Poble Espanyol★
Av. del Marquès de Comillas
☎ **93 325 78 66**
Open Mon. 9am-6pm, Tue.-Thu. 9am-2pm, Fri.-Sat. 9am-4pm, Sun. 9am-6pm. Entry charge.

This 'Spanish Village' was initially conceived for visitors to the 1929 Universal Exhibition as a lightning tour of Spain, but is still just as popular today, representing as it does the diversity of Spanish regional architecture. Folk crafts are on sale in the village and there are restaurants serving regional dishes. Climb to the top of the Torres de Avila to the bar of the same name (see p. 121) for an amazing view.

❹ Estadi Olímpic and Galería★
Avinguda de l'Estadi
Stadium open every day 10am-6pm (8pm in summer). Entry free at Puerta Maraton.
Galería (☎ 93 426 06 60) Open Apr.-Jun. Tue.-Sun. 10am-2pm, 4-7pm; Oct.-Mar. Tue.-Fri. 10am-1pm, 4-6pm; Jul.-Sep. Tue.-Sun. 10am-2pm, 4-8pm. Entry charge at South Gate.

The walls by Pere Domenech date from 1929, and the façade and equestrian sculptures by Gargallo have also been preserved. You can just imagine some 60,000 spectators in full voice cheering the athletes on to victory. In the gallery you can see the costumes created by Els Comediants for the Olympic ceremonies.

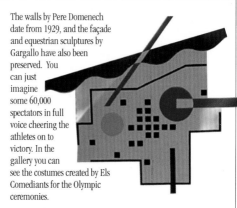

❺ Palau Sant Jordi ★★★
Avinguda de l'Estadi
☎ **93 426 20 89**
Open every day 10am-8pm. Free entry to the Olympic Esplanade.

The Japanese Arata Isozaki made use of state-of-the-art technology when designing the site of the 1992 Olympic gymnastics events. However, nowadays the athletes have been supplanted by showbiz, and rock concerts now call the tune. At sunset, Miyawaki's sculptures create a

beautiful graphic effect – a forest of metallic trees, futuristic creations, are outlined against the sky.

❻ Calatrava tower ★★
Plaça Europa
Free entry.

This space-age telecommunications tower is the elegant counterpoint of the Palau Sant Jordi. It was designed by Santiago Calatrava and dominates the skyline, pointing the way to new horizons.

7 Picornell swimming pools and INEFC★
Avinguda de l'Estadi.

The swimming-pool complex was remodelled for the Olympics and is named after Bernat Picornell, the Catalan swimming pioneer. It rubs shoulders with the neo-Classical building of the Institut Nacional de Educació Fisica de Catalunya (INEFC). The latter, built round a cloister, is typical of its Catalan designer, Ricardo Bofill. The entrance is a portico with Doric columns, like an ancient Greek temple – very impressive, but not particularly innovative. The light-coloured building stands out against a radiant blue sky, once again to grandiose effect.

8 Museu Nacional d'Art de Catalunya (MNAC)★★
Parc Montjuïc
☎ **93 622 03 60**
Open Tue.-Sat. 10am-7pm, Sun. & public hols 10am-2.30pm, closed Mon.
Entry charge.

Symbol of the 1929 Exhibition and recently restored by Gae Aulenti, the former National Palace has housed collections of Catalan art since 1934. Don't miss the superb Roman and Gothic collections. There are remarkable 12th-century frescoes by Urgell and Taüll. This, the best of the art museums in Barcelona, is being renovated and reorganised and in 2003 the collection from the Museu d'Art Modern in Cuitadella park will be moved here.

Opposite the entrance to the amusement park and esplanade, this provides one of the most enjoyable views of the port. The pavement is a collage of ceramic fragments and bottle bases. A sculpture by Subirachs pays 'Homage to Barcelona'. Down below, the Mossen Gardens go cascading down to the port.

9 Mirador de l'Alcalde and Mossen Gardens Costa i Llobrera
Plaça del Mirador
Free entry.

10 Fondació Joan Miró★★★
Parc Montjuïc
☎ **93 329 19 08**
Open Tue.-Sat. 10am-7pm (8pm Jul.-Sep.), Sun. 10am-2.30pm.
Entry charge.

This beautiful white building housing the works of Joan Miró was opened in 1975. Designed by his friend Josep Lluis Sert, it lies in a magical setting in the gardens overlooking the city. The works – paintings, sculptures,

In May 1929, Alphonse XIII inaugurated the Universal Exhibition. It was a showcase for the dictatorship of Primo de Rivera, and only survived him by a few weeks. Most of the buildings you'll see on the hillsides are former pavilions that have been turned into museums or theatres. The Mercat dels Flors theatre, for example, is a strange and ghostly place, but worth a detour.

tapestries and graphics – cover the period 1914-1978 and were donated by Miró himself. There is a restaurant and bookshop.

11 Teatre Grec★
Passeig de l'Exposició.

This reproduction Greek theatre was installed in a disused quarry below the Miró Foundation for the 1929 Exhibition. The quarry's sandstone has been used to build the city since Roman

times. In the Middle Ages porters carried the stone down from Montjuïc for the building of Santa Maria del Mar free of charge. The theatre is now used during the city's cultural festival held in summer. If you can get tickets, an evening watching a performance here as the sun sets, is just magical.

12 Castell de Montjuïc and Military Museum
Summit of Montjuïc Hill
☎ **93 329 86 13**
Open every day except Mon. 9.30am-8pm (summer), 9.30am-4.30pm (winter). Entry charge.

The castle of Montjuïc has witnessed some bloody times. Designed in 1751 in the shape of a star by the engineer Cermeno, it was from here that the city was bombarded in the 1942 rebellion, and five prisoners were executed here by firing squad in 1896. It has

housed the Museu Militar (military history museum) since 1960 and displays fine collections of weaponry, armour, uniforms and maps, as well as portraits of the counts and kings of Catalonia.

Sitges: a short hop to the beach

The fine sandy beaches of the Costa Daurada lie between Barcelona and Tarragona. The seaside resort of Sitges has been spared by developers and retains the elegant character of a turn-of-the century holiday resort, with several *Modernista* villas, a shady palm-fringed *passeig* (promenade), and a church with a pink façade. The resort is perhaps best-known for its pulsating nightlife and is also a popular gay holiday destination. Trains to Sitges depart from Passeig de Gràcia station.

❶ Church square and Passeig de la Ribera★★★

The origins of this once sleepy fishing port are steeped in history. It is said to have been an ancient site and the maritime outlet for the mountain city of Oderdola. The name Sitges is of Iberian

origin and means 'silos' and it is certainly true that stocks of grain have been discovered in hollows carved out of the rock. From the 17th-century church square you can see the promenade which runs the length of the *Platja d'or*.

❷ Museu Cau Ferrat★★

**Carrer Fonollar,
☎ 93 894 03 64
Open in winter: Tue.-Fri. 10am-1.30pm, 3-6.30pm, Sat. 10am-7pm, Sun. 10am-3pm; in summer: Tue.-Sun. 10am-2pm, 5-9pm.
Joint ticket for the three museums (2, 3 and 4)**

In 1893, the astonishing artist and writer Santiago Rusiñol acquired a fisherman's cottage and set up his studio here. His collections of wrought-iron work, ceramics

and Catalan furniture were bequeathed to the city by his widow. See the two works by El Greco that Rusiñol paraded through the streets to parody the Easter procession, and paintings by Picasso, Ramon Casas and Nonell.

❸ Museu Maricel★
For details see Museu Cau Ferrat.

The former city hospital houses a collection of valuable Spanish works of art donated by a collector. The Gothic rooms contain altar-pieces with gold backgrounds and multi-coloured carved wooden sculptures. The entrance hall decorated by Josep Maria Sert (1874-1945), painter of theatrical frescoes and the husband of Mysia, the muse of the Ballets

Russes, is quite a curiosity. On the top floor the Roig collection contains displays of model ships and musical instruments.

❹ Museu Romàntic★
Carrer San Gaudenci, 1
☎ 93 894 29 69
See Museu Cau Ferrat.

This former residence of the Llopis family dates from 1793. The furniture of the period has been preserved, as have the murals by Pau Rigalt tracing the life of the city in the late 18th century. It shows the life of a bourgois family in

---

SANTIAGO RUSIÑOL (1861-1931)

Born of a middle-class family that had made its fortune during the industrial revolution, Rusiñol preferred the Bohemian lifestyle to that of his own class. A fervent Catalan, he travelled abroad regularly and during his stays in Paris cultivated friendships with the painters of Montmartre. He also helped many artists from Barcelona to become known. From 1892 to 1899, Rusiñol organised the *Festes Modernistes*, artistic gatherings of music, painting, sculpture and dance and Sitges became a *Mecca del Modernismo*, or Mecca of Modernism.

---

the 18th and 19th centuries. There is also a collection of delicate old dolls, with pretty hats, little bags, muffs and parasols.

---

❺ and ❻ El Xalet Hotel-Restaurant ★★
Carrer Isla de Cuba, 35
☎ 93 811 00 70
Open May.-Oct. every day 8-11.30pm.

The architect Buigas built this *Modernista* villa in the 19th century. When the *Indianos* – residents who had made their fortune abroad at

the end of the 19th century – returned to the country, they wanted to build luxurious residences. Sitges has a good number of these mansions. Entering the dining room of

the El Xalet is like stepping back in time. You feel as if you should be taking part in a Merchant-Ivory film. Try some of the delicious home cooking prepared by the proprietor (around €24). A double room costs in the region of €54.

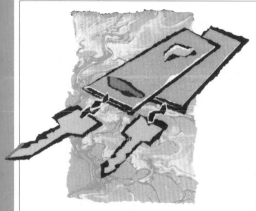

Rooms and restaurants

Practicalities

HOTELS

The city was lacking in luxury hotels before 1992, but since the Olympic Games a good range of accommodation has appeared, with more than 150 hotels meeting the needs of its visitors. If you choose a hotel with sea views, you'll probably find it is in a quiet district, but a long way from the centre. On the other hand, the city centre is noisy and so it's best to ask for a room overlooking a courtyard. You may have a long walk to your hotel as many of them are inaccessible by car.

RATES AND CONDITIONS

The hotels listed in this guide are divided into four categories. The top three categories include telephone, TV and en-suite bathroom; the fourth is more basic. In general, breakfast isn't included in the price of rooms. A supplement is also charged for extra beds for children. There's no distinction between smoking and non-smoking rooms.

Rates for a double room before tax:

★★★★★ from €192

★★★★ between €120 and €192

★★★ between €90 and €120

★★ between €54 and €90

You will be charged an additional 7% tax (*IVA*) per night per room.

If you'd like the complete list of hotels in Barcelona, contact the Barcelona Hotels Association:

Via Laietana 47 (08003),
☎ 93 301 62 40
✆ 93 301 42 92.

You can make reservations in advance by phone or fax. You won't usually be asked for a deposit. However, your room won't be ready until noon at the earliest.

RESTAURANTS

Catalan cuisine tends to be fairly substantial and nourishing, but is not afraid of mixing flavours, so you'll find savoury dishes flavoured with nuts and fruit. As you may imagine from its proximity to the sea, fish and seafood figure heavily in restaurant menus, but meat is also good here. There are essentially three types of eating establishment, the *restaurante* (*restaurant* in Catalan), the *cafetería*, which tends to be cheaper than the restaurants, plus of course you can also order snacks in bars. Most restaurants will have a *menú del día*, or daily set menu. *Tapas* are small dishes of food, which used to be served free with drinks, but for which you now have to pay. *Raciones* are really just bigger portions of *tapas*. A *bodega* (literally 'cellar'), *cerveceria* (*cervesseria* in Catalan), *tasca* (*tasques*) and *taberna* are all types of bar (see p. 13).

In summer, you'll be well advised to make for the port or high parts of the city (Tibidabo) to benefit from any slight breeze, though there are also many shaded terraces in the city centre. Generally speaking, you don't need to book in advance, unless you decide to visit one of the trendiest restaurants, in which case, you can ask your hotel receptionist to book for you. There's no formal dress

code and you can wear whatever you like – a tie isn't compulsory anywhere. However, the people of Barcelona always make every effort to look their best.

'WEEKEND' RATES TO LOOK OUT FOR

Many hotels also operate a *'fin de semana'* price, or 'weekend' rate, which is extremely advantageous, since it allows you a discount of up to 50% of the normal price. It's in your interest to select a higher-category hotel that grants this discount, as you'll pay the same price as you would for an average hotel without discount. Always ask at the time of booking or you can also get information from:

Tourist Information Office

Plaça de Catalunya, 17 (basement)
☎ 93 368 97 30
Open every day 9am-9pm.

This office will help you book a hotel at the *'fin de semana'* rates (operating in 35 selected hotels) and will provide you with a BIP (Barcelona Important Person) card, which gives

you discounts at restaurants, museums, shows, car hire firms, etc. The advantageous *'fin de semana'* prices operate throughout the year at the weekend (Fri.-Sun.), and every day from 21 June to 11 September, and are definitely worth looking out for. There's no need to send payment in advance – you pay the hotel direct. The rates given below are before tax per person for a double room

Category A (★★★★★): around €56

Category B (★★★★): around €42

Category C and D (★★★★) and (★★★): between €24 and €30.

If you're really on a budget, the Tourist Information Office can also advise you of Youth Hostels and student Halls of Residence, some of which take paying guests in summer.

HOTELS

Port Olímpic

Arts Barcelona★★★★★

C. Marina, 19-21, (08005)
☎ 93 221 10 00
🆂 93 221 10 71
Metro Ciutadella
Vila Olímpica.

A hotel beside the sea where businessmen and others find elegant hi-tech rooms and suites with an uninterrupted view of the bay and Port Olímpic. **Bar Terraza** and a swimming pool to top up your suntan.

Eixample

Claris★★★★★

Carrer Pau Claris, 150 (08009)
☎ 93 487 62 62
🆂 93 215 79 70
www.derbyhotels.es
Metro Urquinaona

The former palace of the Counts of Vedruna appeals particularly

to travellers who appreciate its collection of ancient Egyptian artefacts. Each of its 120 rooms is decorated with antiques, paintings and 17th-century English or *Modernista* furniture. There is a private bar.

Ritz★★★★★

Gran Via de les Corts Catalanes, 668 (08010)
☎ 93 318 52 00
🆂 93 318 01 48
Metro Urquinaona.

A delightful place to spend an evening, where Salvador Dalí once demanded a suite for the statue of his horse. A special weekend offer (subject to availability) at this charming, traditional hotel is temptation enough. True to its reputation, a very luxurious hotel.

Alexandra★★★★

Carrer Mallorca, 251 (08008)
☎ 93 467 71 66
🆂 93 488 02 58
Metro Diagonal.

A convenient place to stay close to the city's shops, with 75 wood-decorated designer rooms. A room overlooking the courtyard will give you an idea of the magnificence of the houses in l'Eixample.

Condes de Barcelona★★★★

Pg de Gràcia, 73-75 (08008)
☎ 93 488 22 00
🆂 93 467 47 81
Metro Diagonal.

This *Modernista* building has been brilliantly renovated, preserving the classical Romano-Moorish stairwell and you'll receive a courteous welcome. Ask for a room overlooking the garden at the back of the hotel if you're looking for peace and quiet during your stay.

Duques de Bergara★★★★

Carrer Bergara, 11 (08002)
☎ 93 301 51 51
🆂 93 317 34 42
Metro Catalunya.

You'll love this turn-of-the-century former private mansion, just a stone's throw from Plaça de Catalunya, especially the sumptuous marble entrance and staircase. The convenient car park is a bonus.

Gran Hotel Havana★★★★

Gran Via de les Corts Catalanes, 647 (08010)
☎ 93 412 11 15
🆂 93 412 26 11
Metro Girona.

The hotel's turn-of-the-century façade is reminiscent

of the grand hotels of the seaside resorts of San Sebastian. The 145 rooms, all luxurious, are provided with every comfort – satellite television, air-conditioning, safe, etc. Centrally located and ideal if you like shopping.

St Moritz★★★★

C. Diputación, 262 (08007)
☎ 93 412 15 00
🅕 93 412 12 36
Metro Passeig de Gràcia.

A very central hotel with an interior garden that's a bonus in summer. The neo-Classical façade is impressive, as is the size of the rooms equipped with satellite television. The service is attentive and there's a fitness centre if you have enough energy left after shopping in the neighbouring *passeig*.

Barrio Gòtico

Colon★★★★

Avinguda Catedral, 7 (08002)
☎ 93 301 14 04
🅕 93 317 29 15
Metro Jaume I.

A hotel frequented by Miró opposite the cathedral. Ask for a room with a balcony overlooking the square so that you can follow the movements of the Sunday *sardanas* (Catalan dancing). Its exceptional location is ideal for exploring the Barrio Gòtico.

Regencia Colon★★★

Carrer Sagristans, 13-17 (08002)
☎ 93 318 98 58
🅕 93 317 28 22
Metro Jaume I.

This hotel, a stone's throw from the cathedral, is less luxurious

than the *Colon* (see above) but has the advantage of being in a quiet pedestrian area. It's a good place to come as a family – children can play in the cathedral square.

Metropol★★★

Carrer Ample, 31, (08002)
☎ 93 310 51 00
🅕 93 319 12 76
Metro Jaume I.

Near Port Vell and at the lower end of the Barrio Gòtico, this hotel offers unbeatable value for money. The foyer has retained the character of a private town house, and the rooms are small but secluded. An opportunity you certainly won't want to miss if you're on a budget.

Nouvel★★★

Carrer Santa Anna, 20 (08002)
☎ 93 301 82 74
🅕 93 301 83 70
Metro Catalunya.

The *Modernista* setting of this hotel, a small street in the Barrio Gòtico, isn't lacking in charm. Its carved ceilings, old *azulejos* and elegant stairwell make it a delightful place to stay, especially for visitors who have a particular interest in authentic Art Deco.

Jardi★★★

Plaça Sant Josep Oriol, 1 (08001)
☎ 93 301 59 00
🅕 93 318 36 64
Metro Liceu.

The Jardi is wonderfully located in the beating heart of the city, the Plaça del Pi pedestrian area. The rooms overlook pine trees and street entertainers of all kinds. It's a small but reasonably-priced hotel and our favourite in this category.

Diagonal

Rey Juan Carlos I★★★★★

Av. Diagonal, 661 (08028)
☎ 93 364 40 40
🅕 93 364 42 64
Metro Zona Universitaria.

This was the last hotel to open in 1992 and heads of state from around the world stayed here during the Olympic Games. Its cavernous foyer is impressive, and the 412 rooms are arranged round it as if it were an ocean liner. A little remote from the city centre , however the hotel makes up for this by having room for gardens, terraces and a pool.

Gran Derby★★★★
Carrer Loreto, 28 (08029)
☎ 93 322 20 62
🆏 93 419 68 20
Metro Entença.

To judge from the brick façade, you'd think you were in Chelsea in London, yet the delightful sunlit garden leaves you in little doubt – you are indeed in Barcelona, near the Turò Park district, with its luxurious shop windows. The hotel has ultramodern split-level rooms

and staff will go out of their way to hire cars, and book tickets for concerts and excursions to Montserrat for you.

Ramblas

Rivoli Ramblas★★★★
La Rambla, 128 (08002)
☎ 93 302 66 43
🆏 93 318 87 60
Metro Catalunya.

At the top of the Ramblas, this 1930s building, restored in an original way, has given each of its 90 rooms a distinctive touch – antique dealers, young designers and artists were involved in the project. Very good location, but no car park.

Méridien Barcelona★★★
La Rambla, 111 (08002)
☎ 93 318 62 00
🆏 93 301 77 76
Metro Catalunya.

This hotel, in the heart of the Ramblas, is a favourite with celebrities, including Michael Jackson, Bruce Springsteen, The Rolling Stones, Oasis and Placido Domingo. It has 206 comfortable and sophisticated rooms offering all the facilities a star could want.

Mercure Barcelona Rambla★★★
La Rambla, 124 (08002)
☎ 93 412 04 04
🆏 93 318 73 27
Metro Catalunya.

Ideally located in the Ramblas, this hotel is a strategic starting point for walks in the Barrio Gòtico and Raval. There are 76 convenient rooms located behind the turn-of-the-century façade, and a foyer with a new designer look. Very friendly reception.

Raval

Sant Agusti★★★
Plaça Sant Agusti, 3 (08001)
☎ 93 318 16 58
🆏 93 317 29 28
Metro Liceu.

In a shady, peaceful square close to the Ramblas, the Sant Agusti hotel is situated beside St Augustine's church. Ask for the attic rooms, with exposed beams, which are quite delightful. There's a handy car park in the area too.

España★★

C. Sant Pau, 9-11 (08001)
☎ 93 318 17 58
📠 93 317 11 34
Metro Liceu.

To fans of Art Nouveau, the dining rooms designed by Domenech i Montaner are quite irresistible. Set in the heart of the Barrio Chino, the España keeps alive memories of a bygone age – but the decor in the dining room is really more memorable than the food. The bedrooms are spacious and comfortable. Ask for a room overlooking the lovely indoor patio if possible.

Sitges

San Sebastian★★★★

Port Alegre, 53 (08870)
☎ 93 894 86 76
📠 93 894 04 30.

Opposite the small bay of San Sebastian, the hotel's fifty-one spruce rooms are both pleasant and practical. With the sunny terrace inviting you to relax and enjoy your stay, it's just the place to satisfy your longing for idleness and the beach (see pp. 68-69).

El Xalet★★

C. Isla de Cuba, 35 (08870)
☎ 93 811 00 70
📠 93 894 55 79.

This beautifully preserved *Modernista* villa is set in a luxuriant garden with a pool. The ten rooms are furnished with a rather motley collection of furniture. The friendly welcome and food prepared from fresh market produce, lovingly prepared by the owner are sure to please those seeking a quiet setting.

Romàntic★★

Carrer Sant Isidre, 33 (08870)
☎ 93 894 83 75
📠 93 894 81 67
Closed in winter .

Three *Modernista* houses were saved to create this hotel, pictured below. Visitors can enjoy the patio, planted with palm trees, and share the owner's nostalgia for Modernisme. Ask for a peaceful room with a balcony overlooking the garden for the lovely view.

RESTAURANTS

Barrio Gòtico

Hostal El Pintor★★

Carrer St Honorat, 7
☎ 93 301 40 65
Metro Jaume I
Open every day.

This hotel is pleasantly situated behind the cathedral, with the emphasis on trendy decor – exposed bricks and beams and gleaming floor-tiles. They serve traditional Catalan cuisine – asparagus with marinated salmon, and hake with leeks grilled the old-fashioned way.

El Gran Café★

Carrer d'Avinyò, 9
☎ 93 318 79 86
Metro Liceu
Closed Sun. and public holidays.

El Gran Café's copper coffee percolator, black and white checked floor tiles, bistrot tables and starched tablecloths, put you in mind of fin-de-siecle Paris. Senor Ramon will be only to pleased to show you his connoisseur's wine cellar (*bodega*), if you ask him. The set lunch is €7.20.

Pou Dols★★

Baixada de Sant Miquel, 6
☎ 93 412 05 79
Open Mon.-Sat.

Pou Dols menu is varied and delicious – consommé with

liver mousse, sardine tart with young garlic, white fish with parmesan, and boned pig's trotters with artichokes. With an inventive menu and a sober decor by Starck and Maurer, this is currently a very popular place. After sampling some of these gourmet dishes you will doubtless be added to its list of fans. Not far from the *Ajuntament* (Town Hall). Allow around €24 per person.

Eixample

Casa Calvet★★★

Carrer de Casp, 48
☎ 93 412 40 12
Metro Urquinaona
Closed Sun. & public hols.

Set in one of the houses built by Gaudí (see p. 30), which used to house a textile business, Casa Calvet resembles a loft with wooden beams and traditionally stuccoed walls. Among the chef's recommendations are tasty cockle salad,

delicious fresh lasagne with scampi, melting fillet of sole with cava, and mouth-watering white chocolate mousse.

Semproniana★★

Carrer de Rosselló, 148
☎ 93 453 18 20
Metro Diagonal.

This former printing factory offers a charming setting for diners in a cosy candlelit atmosphere amongst antique furniture. The creative Catalan cuisine includes black sausage lasagne and 'Delirium Tremens' – a wonderfully wicked chocolate dessert.

Madrid-Barcelona★★★

Carrer d'Aragò, 282
☎ 93 215 70 26
Metro Passeig de Gràcia
Closed Sun. and public hols.

Not very far from the Tàpies foundation, this former railway station has been converted into a *tapas* bar serving omelettes, squid and aubergines (eggplants) – with a slice of nostalgia thrown in.

Flash-Flash★

Granada del Penedès, 25
☎ 93 237 09 90
Open every day 1pm-1am.
Metro Diagonal.

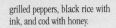

A popular meeting spot for trendy Barcelona society, Flash-Flash is a rather glamorous venue, decorated with black-and-white photos and pop art. Enjoy a selection of omelettes or the best hamburgers in town. The service is faultless, and the post-midnight 'Menu Golfo' is good value at €9.02.

Port and Barceloneta

Els Pescadors★★★

Plaça Prim, 1
☎ 93 225 20 18
Metro Poble Nou
Open every day.

This terrace beyond the Olympic Village is a delightful place to enjoy the mild air. Opt for the marble-tabled 'antigua' room rather than the more impersonal 'moderna', and try oven-grilled peppers, black rice with ink, and cod with honey.

Barceloneta★★

L'Escar, 22 Moll dels Pescadors
☎ 93 221 21 11
Metro Barceloneta
Open every day.

For armchair sailors. Wood, rope and coarse sail-cloth create a nautical atmosphere in this fashionable restaurant overlooking Port Vell. Picture windows, duckboards, wood panelling and red and blue striped canvas tablecloths help to whet the appetite as surely as the sea air.

Cal Pinxo★★

Carrer de Baluard, 124
Platja Barceloneta
☎ 93 221 50 28
Metro Barceloneta
Closed Sun. evening and Mon.

With *chiringuitos* (see p. 61) a thing of the past, the Cal Pinxo restaurant carries on the tradition of the kiosks and fishermen's restaurants, serving *fideus a la cassola*, *paella* with pasta, *mariscos*, seafood and monkfish in *cazuela* with ailloli sauce.

Carballeira★★

C. de Reina Cristina 3
☎ 93 310 10 06
Metro Barceloneta
Closed Sun. evening, Mon. and public holidays.

An excellent fish restaurant that makes no concessions to fashion. Plenty of local colour, with portholes, model ships and turtles – an endearing popular classic according to some, an affront according to others. Judge for yourself!

Reial Club Marítim★★

Moll d'Espanya,
☎ 93 221 62 56
Metro Barceloneta
Closed Sun. evening.

Turning its back on the hi-tech Maremagnum, this little place is like an officers' club from another era. The view of the overhead bridge, *Rambla de Mar*, and the steamers setting off for the islands only adds to the atmosphere, and the culinary delights – bass in rosemary, fish soup and pasta with prawns – are wonderful.

The city heights

A Contraluz ★★

C. del Milanesat, 19 (not on map – near Via Augusta, off C. Doctor Roux)
☎ 93 203 06 58
Take a taxi
Open every day.

The setting and summer terrace of this Tragaluz restaurant (see p. 53) will make you forget the city. Try the delicious risotto with boletus mushrooms, foie gras with baby onions, or potato and vine-leaf puffs. As in most restaurants, you can try this tasty Catalan cuisine more cheaply from the lunch menu (€13.80).

Can Travi Nou★★

Cami Antic de Sant Cebrià
☎ 93 428 03 01
Take a taxi
Closed Sun. evening.

This Catalan property in the city heights has the look of a family home. A climbing vine twines round the pergola, where the guests sit and savour the delights of country cooking. If you warm to Latin charm, give your order to the Brylcreemed waiter.

El Asador de Aranda★★

Avinguda del Tibidabo, 31
☎ 93 417 01 15
Avinguda Tibidabo rail stn.
Closed Sun. evening.

You come here for the decor – the Moorish entrance to this *Modernista* house is like a harem. In summer, on the terrace, they invariably serve shoulder of lamb grilled in an old-fashioned charcoal oven. Before leaving, climb the tower for the unique view.

La Balsa★★

C. de la Infanta Isabel, 4
☎ 93 211 50 48
Avinguda Tibidabo rail stn.
Closed Sun. and Mon.

A restaurant nestling on the Tibidabo hillside, with a straw awning that complements the greenery. Designed by Tusquets, it won a prize in 1979. With comfortable sofas and a choice of books, it's a delightfully relaxing place.

Try the hake tartare and red-fruit sorbet which are as light as air.

Atlantic Restaurant★★

Av. Luis Montades, 8
☎ 93 418 52 04
Open Mon.-Sat.

The first of the Atlantic's two main advantages is its marvellous view over the Mediterranean. Add to this a menu full of sophisticated flavours and you won't regret having come this far. There are mussels stuffed with liver, rice with clams, sole stuffed with prawns in oyster sauce, and *magrets de canard* with raspberries (€30-42).

La Venta★★

Plaça del Doctor Andreu,
☎ 93 212 64 55
Closed Sun. Take a taxi.

This pastel-coloured open-air café perched on top of the Tibidabo still has a late 19th-century air and old-fashioned charm. It's the ideal place for couples, who can huddle up to the stove in winter or dream on the terrace in summer while sharing a *matò de panses amb melles*, a sweet made from honey and currants .

Bonanova★

Carrer de Sant Gervasi de Cassoles, 103
☎ 93 417 10 33
Plaça J. Folguera rail stn
Closed Sun. evening and Mon.

This family restaurant is reminiscent of a 1900's gaming

room. The *Modernista* decor of coloured *azulejos*, black and white tiled floor and tarnished mirrors hasn't aged a bit. From rabbit and snails to tasty fried fish, the menu wavers between land and sea. Worth the detour!

Ribera

Cal Pep★★

Plaça de les Olles, 8
☎ 93 319 61 83
Metro Jaume I
Closed Sun. and Mon. lunch.

At Ribera you have to stand at the *barra* (bar) to try out the chef's various suggestions. He concocts fried food and dishes of the day – *supions* and *tellines*, *pulpitos* and shellfish – right before your eyes. A slice of life to savour!

El Salero★

Carrer del Rec, 60
☎ 93 319 80 22
Closed Sat. & Sun.
Metro Jaume 1

The trendy and chic frequent this café/bar/restaurant, with

its 'New York' style interior and relaxed atmosphere. The white decor is dotted with objects found in London flea markets, and there's a very cosmopolitan atmosphere. Enjoy tasty tartares, desserts, salads and excellent music.

Future★★

Carrer Fusina, 5
☎ 93 319 92 99
Open Mon.-Sat. 8.30am-11pm.

This loft, with its rather severe decor of white bricks and aluminium bar, is the latest place to see and be seen. Try the bar menu — we recommend the vegetable lasagne in a tomato and goat's cheese sauce. If you're planning a round of the bars in Plaça Del Born, currently the in-district, it's the ideal place to start.

Raval

Casa Leopoldo★★★

Carrer de Sant Rafael, 24
☎ 93 441 30 14
Closed Sun. evening and Mon.
Metro Liceu.

In rooms decorated with yellow and blue *azulejos*, you'll be served the best *pà amb tomaquet* (see p. 10) in the city, as well as fried young fish, prawns and scampi. The customary presence of famous writers Vázquez Montalbán,

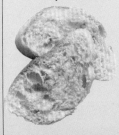

Marsé, and Mendoza may explain the dubious relation between cost and quality. Perhaps it's the price of fame.

Ramblas

La Véronica★

Carrer d'Avinyò, 30
☎ 93 412 11 22
Open Wed.-Sun. noon-1am,
Tue. 8pm-1.30am.
Metro Liceu

Noisy and fashionable, this restaurant and pizzeria is a great people-watching spot. The food is surprisingly good and includes Gorgonzola and apple flavoured pizzas, tasty quiches and delicious desserts.

Quinze Nits★

Plaça Reial, 6
☎ 93 317 30 75
Metro Drassanes
Open every day.

Living on its reputation of good quality, price and location, under the arches of the Plaça Reial, this popular venue is not as good as it once was. The €5.98 menu is still one of the better deals around, however, but be prepared to queue.

Barceloneta

Agua★★

Passeig Marítim de la Barceloneta, 30
☎ 93 206 06 58
Open lunchtime: Mon.-Fri. 1.30-4pm (to 5pm Sat. &

Sun.); evenings: Mon.-Sun. 8.30pm-midnight (to 1am Fri. & Sat.).
Metro Barceloneta.

This is an idyllic spot, with its sea-and-sky-blue decor, for an apéritif or fresh seafood, simply prepared. There's a pleasant atmosphere, a delightful sea view at lunchtime and a romantic ambience at night under the stars.

Sitges

Maricel ★★

Passeig de la Ribera, 6
☎ 93 894 20 54.
Closed Tue. evening and Wed.

On the *paseo* (promenade) facing the bay, the terrace between sea and sky (*mar i cel* – hence the name) Maricel serves classic Mediterranean cuisine – *paella marinera*, with fresh fish, *escalivada*, sweet peppers, aubergines (eggplants), and onions marinated in olive oil.

CAFÉS AND TEAROOMS

Ciutadella

Hivernacle Café

Parc de la Ciutadella
Passeig Picasso
☎ 93 295 40 17
Metro Ciutadella
Open Mon.-Sat. 10am-
midnight, Sun. 10am-5pm.

A greenhouse dating from the Great Exhibition of 1888 has become the most romantic summer garden café, with

luxuriant plants, purring cats and even a melodious fountain which echoes the live jazz which is played there on Wednesdays.

Ramblas

Bar Jardin

Carrer de la Portaferissa, 17
Metro Liceu.

Take me to the Casbah! A camel and oasis create an exotic atmosphere. There are also little garden tables and pop-art sofas which all add up to an interesting mix of styles and a haven for the young.

Raval

Granja Viader

Carrer d'En Xuclà, 4
☎ 93 318 34 86
Metro Catalunya
Closed Sun. and Mon.
morning.

Granja has found the formula for a tearoom to please all ages, from children to little old ladies, and from creative types to people laden with shopping bags. Here's where you'll find the best crème brûlée, Swiss chocolate with whipped cream and homemade lemon madeleines in the city.

Horchateria Sirvent

Carrer de Parlament, 56
☎ 93 441 27 20
Metro Sant Antoni
Open every day.

Slake your thirst near the Ronda San Pau with *horchata*, barley water, or a *turròn*-flavoured ice cream (see p. 113). People traditionally hesitate between *granizada*, coffee-flavoured, crushed ice, and a delicious ice-cream cornet. You can worry about your diet tomorrow!

Barrio Gòtico

Bon Mercat

Baixada de la Llibreteria, 1-3
☎ 93 315 29 08
Metro Jaume I.
Closed Sun.

For €0.57, you can savour a strong black coffee, or *tallat* with a dash of milk, with the heady aroma of Guatemalan coffee, Ethiopian mocca or *gran altura mezcla*. Drink your choice standing at the crowded bar with a tasty *bocadillo*.

El Taxidermista

Plaça Reial, 8
☎ 93 317 06 97
Metro Liceu
Open Tue.-Sun. 10am-
2.30am (closed Mon.).

The former natural history museum has been extensively and successfully renovated and now houses a remarkable café and restaurant with a cosmopolitan atmosphere and a sophisticated, intellectual clientèle. The interior is a subtle mix of *modernista* and contemporary design, and it's a good spot for breakfast, a selection of tapas or an appetizing Mediterranean meal. You'll receive a friendly welcome and enjoy a great view of Plaça Reial. Lunch menus range from €6-7.20.

Bar del Pi

Plaça Sant Josep Oriol, 1
☎ 93 302 21 23
Metro Liceu
Open every day.

The Plaça del Pi is the most pleasant and charming terrace in the city. Intellectuals, the 'divine left', and artists short of inspiration come here. Newspapers are available for customers to read and the noise of the coffee percolator makes a change from the sounds of jazz in the square.

El Café d'Estiu

Plaça Sant Iu, 5
☎ 93 310 30 14
Metro Jaume I
Open every day 7-10pm
(except Mon.).

In summer, a few tables are set up near a refreshing pool in the courtyard of the F. Marès museum, in the heart of the Barrio Gotico. Large white parasols and a wooden stall offer visitors a delicious break in a quiet haven.

Eixample

Laie

Pau Claris, 85
☎ 93 318 17 39
Metro Urquinaona
Mon.-Fri. 10am-9pm, Sat. 10.30am-9pm.

For a literary and gourmet break, this tearoom-cum-bookshop is a dream come true. Magazines from all over the world, art books and philosophical treatises mingle with home-made pastries and the smell of coffee. A perfect blend of nourishment for body and soul.

Mauri

Rambla de Catalunya, 103
☎ 93 215 09 98
Metro Diagonal
Open every day
(closed Sun. 3-5pm).

Smart young mothers with babies and well-dressed ladies come here to indulge their sweet tooth. A confectioners and cake shop where perfect taste, elaborate display shelves and black and gold window displays are the order of the day.

Sitges

La Estrella Sitges

Carrer Major, 52
☎ 93 894 00 79
Closed Mon.

This patisserie is decorated from floor to ceiling with frescoes, bottles of liqueur and boxes of sweets. Traditional treats await you in the *salò de t*é –

why not try a little glass of Sitges malmsey, the local liqueur, as well?

Ribera

El Xampanyet

Carrer de Montcada, 22
☎ 93 319 70 03
Metro Jaume I
Open Tue.-Sat. noon-4pm, 6.30-11.30pm, Sun. 6.30-11.30pm.

A small, friendly inn run by the same family since 1929 Colourful *azulejos*, flasks and wine barrels set the tone. The anchovies, olives, and marinated fish served with Penedès white wine are delicious, but watch the bill.

Shopping Practicalities

The people of Barcelona have a nose for business – hardly surprising since the city was founded on commerce, and trading has taken place here for 2,000 years – so no need to worry, there are shops on every street corner.

The most stylish shops (selling jewellery, designer labels and luxury clothes) are on the Passeig de Gràcia, Rambla de Catalunya and in the area around the Turò park. Arts and crafts and small businesses liven up the old quarters (Barrio Gòtico and Ribera), the Boqueria market on the Ramblas opens very early in the morning and the port attracts many shoppers as well with the new

FINDING YOUR WAY

Next to each address in the Shopping and Nightlife sections we have given its location on the map of Barcelona on pages 82-83.

Maremagnum centre, which is also open on Sundays.

SHOP OPENING HOURS

Most shops open Monday to Saturday, 10am to 2pm and 4.30 to 8pm, with food shops opening an hour earlier in the morning. Make a note of the opening hours if you don't want to get caught out – all the shops close for lunch, with the exception of the big shopping centres, Illà on the Diagonal and Corte Inglès in the Plaça de Catalunya, which stay open all day long. Some shops close on Saturday afternoons, but the Maremagnum shopping centre located in the port is open from 11am to 11pm.

PAYING FOR YOUR PURCHASES

Most shopkeepers accept credit cards (American Express, Mastercard and Visa International) and, of course, cash. You just present your card and sign the till receipt in the usual way. In the event of loss or theft, call the relevant centre in Madrid:

American Express
☎ 91 572 03 03
🇫 91 570 19 97
Diners
☎ 91 701 59 00
🇫 91 523 32 03
Mastercard and Visa
☎ 91 519 21 00
🇫 91 346 54 43.

Traveller's cheques are commonly accepted. You can also pay with Eurocheques in some establisments.

SALES

The majority of shops hold their sales from the second week in January to the end of February and in July and August. They're not as spectacular as the London sales but you can usually find reductions of anything from 25 to 50%, except at Zara (clothes), where the prices are really slashed.

Prices are displayed everywhere and it isn't done to bargain apart from in flea-markets, where you'll find that the Catalans are tough negotiators and every penny counts. So, be firm, forewarned is forearmed! You can apply for a visitor's shopping card (see p. 35) from:

Turisme de Barcelona
Plaça de Catalunya, 17 (basement)
☎ 93 368 97 30
www.barcelonaturisme.com
This card provides certain benefits (including discounts of around 10%) in more than 200 shops where the sign '*Barcelona, ciutat de compres*' ('Barcelona, the shoppers' paradise') is displayed in the window. Worth getting if you're planning to do a lot of shopping!

for a '*Tax-free cheque*' when making your purchase. On leaving Spain, make sure you have the 'cheques' stamped at customs so that you can cash them at a branch of the Banco Exterior de España when you arrive home. If you buy a work of art or antique declared as *de valor patrimonial* ('of national value'), you must request an export licence from the Spanish equivalent of the National Heritage. The vendor will help you with this process. You can insist on a certificate of authenticity. An invoice is always essential – you can be asked for it at customs and it will be useful to you if you want to sell your purchase at a later date, or if you're burgled and need to fill in a claim form for your insurance company. Be on the lookout

TRANSPORT FACILITIES

If you buy a piece of furniture or bulky object, there's no problem about having it delivered home. Simply give the delivery company a photocopy of your invoice, and they'll make out the delivery note.
UPS, United Parcel Service freephone
☎ 900 10 24 10
www.ups.com
This haulier makes deliveries worldwide and can arrange immediate dispatch if required.

Seur Internacional
☎ 93 263 26 22
www.seurinternacional.com
This leading Spanish delivery company delivers packages to all European capitals in 24 hours, United States in 48 hours and the rest of the world in under 96 hours.

for forgeries and stolen goods. If you export one of the latter, you could be prosecuted for possession of stolen goods. Buy only from established traders and be wary of anything that looks too much of a bargain.
Customs:
Passeig Josep Carner 27,
☎ 93 443 30 08.

CUSTOMS DUTY ON PURCHASES

If you're a citizen of a member state of the European Union, you won't have to pay any customs duty on your purchases, whatever their value, but you will have to show the receipts. Non EU-citizens are exempt from paying VAT on purchases with a value of more than €90.15. Remember to ask

WOMEN'S FASHION: READY-TO-WEAR, ACCESSORIES, SHOES AND DESIGNER CLOTHES

You may dream of being a *Barefoot Contessa*, or stealing the show in *High Society*. You may aspire to taking *Breakfast at Tiffany's*, whilst in search of *La Dolce Vita*, but if if you find yourself attending *Four Weddings and a Funeral* you will certainly need some *Pret-à-Porter*. Cinematic fantasies apart, if you'd like to inject a little Spanish style into your wardrobe, here are some places to try.

Forum

C. de Ferlandina, 31 (C2)
☎ 93 441 80 18
Open Tue.-Sat.
10.30am-2pm,
5-8.30pm

Just a step away from the Museum of Contemporary Art, the work of sixty jewellery designers is on display in this workshop/ gallery and shop which is run by a young German woman. The stunning pieces are made in limited editions and prices range from €24-600. If you're a lover of unique, contemporary jewellery, make sure you come here, and don't forget to take a look at the workshop to see how it's all made.

Muxart

C. de Rosselló, 230 (C/D1)
☎ 93 488 10 64
Open Mon.-Sat.
10am-2pm, 4.30-8.30pm.

Muxart is an outstanding Catalan designer who excels in the art of making boots and ankle boots, both with and without laces. Made in Minorca, they're distinctive for the detail of the finish and the quality of the materials. If you're looking for originality you've come to the right place. Expect to pay €120-138.

Loewe

Passeig de Gràcia, 35 (C1/2)
☎ 93 216 04 00
Metro Passeig de Gràcia
Open Mon.-Sat. 9.30am-8pm.

Loewe uses the elegant façade of the Casa Lléo Morera as a setting for its luxury leather goods. Like its first cousins Gucci and Hermès, Loewe supplies top of the range goods. With its 150-year tradition of quality and luxury, the company has all the know-how needed to produce stylish, distinctive leather articles and colourful, elegant silk scarves.

Groc

C. de Muntaner, 385 ((C1/2)
☎ 93 202 30 77
Open Mon.-Sat. 10am-2pm,
4.30-8.30pm.

One of the first places to have sold
clothes by designers such as
Antonio Miró, for both men and
women. Groc has introduced its
own label and offers a choice of
sophisticated, elegant garments
made of cotton, linen and silk in
fluid simple shapes and designs.

Casa Oliveras

C. de la Dagueria, 11 (off map)
☎ 93 315 19 05
Metro Jaume I
Open Mon.-Fri. 9am-1pm,
4-7pm.

Who says Catalan embroidery has
gone out of style? Behind the
cathedral, in a shop with unusual
porcelain lampshades, Rosa
embroiders decorative detail that
will give ordinary dresses a
somewhat antique look.

El Mercadillo

C. de la Portaferissa, 17 (C2)
☎ 93 317 85 64
Metro Catalunya
Open Mon.-Sat. 10.30am-
8pm.

With a cardboard camel and New
Age music to greet you, you'll
know you're in an unusual shop.
The owner sells a combination of
streetwear, casual clothes and
secondhand items, including a
cool look for psychedelic evenings
– platform shoes, fluorescent
skirts, ponchos and shirts made of
African fabrics – to suit those who
like to be a little different.

Casa Ciutad

Avinguda del Portal de
l'Angel, 14 (C2)
☎ 93 317 04 33
Open Mon.-Fri. 10.30am-
9pm, Sat. 10am-9pm.

Since 1892, the company has
supplied *articulos de tocador*
(toiletry articles), including a
formidable array of brushes and
combs, some of them Spanish-
style, to hold complicated hairdos
in place (€21-84).

Lydia Delgado

C. de Minerva, 21 (C1)
☎ 93 415 99 98
Metro Diagonal
Open Mon.-Fri. 9am-2pm,
4.30-8.30pm, Sat. 10am-
2pm, 4.30-8.30pm.

This young Spanish designer
shows her chic, sexy clothes in a

LA MANUAL ALPARGATERA

Carrer d'Avinyò, 7
☎ 93 301 01 72
Metro Liceu
Open Mon.-Sat. 9.30am-
1.30pm, 4.30-8pm.

B ehind a whitewashed façade
lie espadrilles of every
different shape and size – boot-
style, with laces or embroidery,
coloured and striped. The
workshop is on the premises
and you can order a pair made-
to-measure from the owner,
who supplies the likes of Jack
Nicholson and Pope John Paul
II. You can even buy some
mini-espadrilles for a new baby
(€3-3.60)?

1950s setting, with suits priced
from €600, as well as 1960s
Cubist dresses and hipster trousers
– all up-to-date styles as dynamic
as their designer.

Julie Sohn

C. de Consell de Cent, 308 (D2)
☎ 93 487 84 24
Open Mon.-Sat. 10.30am-8.30pm.

Julie Sohn, a young Korean designer creates demure styles more reminiscent of Jil Sander than Jean-Paul Gaultier. Made in Barcelona, the raw wool suits and poplin shirts create a no-frills, trendy traditional look (a suit costs €360-430).

Josep Font Luz Diaz

Passeig de Gràcia, 106 (C1/2)
☎ 93 415 65 50
Metro Diagonal
Open Mon.-Sat. 10am-8pm.

Long, pure, fluid lines and earthy shades, brown and black add a touch of sophistication to the collections of these two Catalan designers. Elegant women who like pared-down designs will find plain fabrics enhanced with beautiful patterns in the weave, or simple, discreet accessories.

Joieria Sunyer

Gran Via de les Corts Catalanes, 660
☎ 93 317 22 93
Metro Urquinaona
Open Mon.-Fri. 10am-1.30pm, 4.30-8pm.

Since 1835, five generations of jewellers have succeeded one another in this Art Deco setting opposite the Ritz, a magnificent showcase for gilded silver bracelets (€360) and jewellery in exclusive designs passed down from father to son. A custom jewellers providing an old-fashioned service.

Notémon

C. de Pau Claris, 159 (C1)
☎ & ☏ 93 487 60 84
Metro Passeig de Gràcia
Open Tue.-Sat. 10.30am-2pm, 4.30-8.30pm, closed Mon. & Sun.

You'll find a selection of modern clothes for both men and women in this original shop, with its light and airy and white interior. The collections range from classic to the latest styles, and even vintage. The choice is up to you.

Jean Pierre Bua

Av. Diagonal, 469 (C/D1)
☎ 93 439 71 00
Metro Diagonal
Open Mon.-Sat. 10am-2pm, 4.30-8.30pm.

With sexy layering, sophisticated recycling and scandalous see-throughs, this shop offers chic or ethnic, classic, retro or modern styles. Designers such as Sybilla, Jean-Paul Gaultier, Marcel Marougiu, Jean Colonna, Yamamoto and Vivienne Westwood are here to give you an unusual and glamorous new look.

Zara

Avinguda del Portal de l'Angel, 24
☎ 93 301 29 25
Metro Catalunya
Avinguda Diagonal, 584
☎ 93 414 29 46
Metro Diagonal
Pelai, 58
☎ 93 301 09 78
Metro Catalunya
Rambla de Catalunya, 67
☎ 93 487 08 18
Metro Passeig de Gràcia
Open Mon.-Sat. 10am-9pm.

Zara is the latest brand of Spanish clothes. Its popular range of men's, women's and children's lines are inexpensive versions of the latest looks on the high street and are made in good quality fabrics. In a pale wood setting, and with styles ranging from basic to trendy, you'll find sweaters from about €30 and summer suits for €96.

Cristina Castañer

C. del Mestre Nicolau, 23 (B/C1)
☎ 93 414 24 28
C. de València, 274 (C1)
☎ 93 487 21 62
Open Mon.-Sat. 10.30am-2.30pm, 4.30-8pm.

Cristina has inherited the house of Castañer, famous for many years for the quality and design of its traditional espadrilles. She launches two new collections each year – in summer her

Hipòtesi

Rambla de Catalunya, 105 (C1)
☎ 93 215 02 98
Metro Passeig de Gràcia
Open Mon. & Sat. 10am-1.30pm, 5-8.30pm, Tue.-Fri. 10am-8.30pm.

Even the window display is a little gem in this jewellery shop, which

range features cotton and jute espadrilles in unusual shapes, styles and colours and in winter the collection boasts shoes made from leather with a '1950s revisited' feel.

sets itself apart from others with its innovative collection of pieces in such diverse materials as ceramics, glass and fabric. If you love jewellery, it would be a real shame to miss it.

Rafa Teja Atelier

C. de Santa Maria, 18 (D1)
☎ 93 310 27 85

C. del Comte de Salvatierra, 10 (C1)
☎ 93 237 70 59
Open Mon.-Fri. 10am-2pm, 4.30-8.30pm, Sat. 10am-2pm.

The designs in this shop combine contemporary design and handmade quality, with beautiful scarves made of natural fabrics such as silk, cotton and wool. They are hand-painted and embroidered in India, and are available in a wonderful range of colours and materials.

LOVE AT FIRST SIGHT...

ROSER Y FRANCESC

C. de València, 285 (C1)
☎ 93 459 14 53
Metro Passeig de Gràcia
Open Mon.-Sat. 10am-2pm, 4.30-8.30pm (closed Sun.).

There's an intimate atmosphere and a retro feel to this spot, in stark contrast to the resolutely modern clothes. You'll receive a warm welcome before you browse through local and international designs by Antonio Miró, Josep Abril, Ailanto Kenzo, Tara Jarmon and Locking Shockings.

MEN'S FASHION

Men's fashion in Barcelona comes in every possible shape and form. Whatever style you go for – formal or casual, classic or trendy, intellectual or sporty, Latin lover or cool dude – you'll find clothes to suit you in this selection of shops.

lies in the textures he achieves using the latest technology. The cuts are simple, elegant and comfortable for those wanting a 'Bohemian Chic' look.

El Transwaal
C. de l'Hospital, 67 (C3)
☎ 93 301 91 18
Metro Liceu
Open Mon.-Sat.
9.30am-2pm, 4.30-8pm.

Adolfo Dominguez
Passeig de Gràcia, 32 (C1/2)
☎ 93 487 41 70
Passeig de Gràcia, 89 (C1/2)
☎ 93 215 13 39
Av. Diagonal, 490 (C/D1)
☎ 93 416 11 92
Open Mon.-Sat. 10am-8pm.

If you're planning a business meeting or romantic dinner with the woman in your life, the collections of this internationally-famous designer are absolutely not to be missed. High-quality fabrics and natural colours give Dominguez' refined clothes a sober elegance.

A shop that's worth the visit for the sign alone. A shop-window dummy in a starched hat welcomes you to a world of professional uniforms, including a waiter's dinner suit and chef's

David Valls
C. de València, 235 (C1)
☎ 93 487 12 85
Open Mon.-Sat. 10am-2pm, 5-8.30pm.

David Valls experiments and innovates and like most of his creative contemporaries in Barcelona, he uses different fabrics (wool, silk and cotton) in a very personal way. His originality

outfit. Ideal for impressing the guests at your next dinner party.

Camper

**Centre Commercial
el Triangle
C. de Pelai 13-37 (C2)
☎ 93 302 41 24
Open Mon.-Sat.
10.30am-10pm.**

In the newly-built shopping centre in the Plaça de Catalunya, you'll get off on the right foot with Camper's crepe soles and colourful supple leathers. Innovative shoe designs for everyone.

Furest

**Av. Diagonal, 468 (B/C1)
☎ 93 416 06 65
Passeig de Gràcia, 12-14 (C2)
☎ 93 301 20 00
Open Mon.-Sat. 10am-2pm,
4.30-8pm.**

This temple to sartorial elegance has been selling classic designs for men for many generations. Clothes range from tailored suits to casual and sportswear, and the collections are sophisticated and top quality.

Gonzalo Comella

**Av. Diagonal, 478 (C/D1)
☎ 93 416 15 16
Metro Diagonal
Open Mon.-Sat. 10am-
8.30pm.
Passeig de Gràcia, 6 (C1/2)
☎ 93 412 66 00
Metro Catalunya
Open Mon.-Sat. 10am-9pm.**

You'll find fashionable clothes for both town and country, including parkas by A. Miró , Ralph Lauren pullovers, Hugo Boss suits, Armani shirts and Church's shoes.

Ovlas Men

**C. de la Portaferissa, 25, (C2)
☎ 93 412 52 29
Metro Liceu
Open every day 10am-2pm,
4.30-8.30pm.**

Drainpipe or hipster trousers, close-fitting jackets and Chairman Mao shirts – 1960s-style menswear for those who don't want to wear Levi's. With trousers made from stretchy material, sexy satin shirts and toreador-style jackets, you're bound to cut a quite considerable dash on the dance floor.

Sombreria Obach

**C. del Call, 2 (C3)
☎ 93 318 40 94
Metro Liceu
Open Mon.-Fri.
9.30am-1.30pm, 4-8pm,
Sat. 4.30-8pm.**

In the heart of the old town, Sombreria Obach have been making hats for three generations. Take your pick from caps (€6-24), Basque berets (*boinas*, €12), *barretina catalana* – Catalan caps that are worn pulled down

CHILDREN'S CLOTHES AND GAMES

In a country with one of the lowest birth rates in Europe it isn't surprising that children are treated like royalty. Like the Italians, the Spanish have always loved children and you will find that they are readily accepted in most places. Here are some suggestions for places to spoil your own.

El Rey de la Magia
C. de la Princesa, 11 (D3)
☎ 93 319 39 20
Metro Jaume I
Open Mon.-Fri. 10am-2pm, 5-8pm (closed Sat. pm).

Everything for children who want to be magicians when they grow up. Jokes and tricks of every kind, including conjuring tricks and sleight-of-hand, that are just the thing for the budding magician. With a blood-red shop-window display and a sign in the form of a turbaned genie with a hypnotic stare, be prepared to fall under its spell.

Juguetes Foyé
C. dels Banys Nous, 13 (C3)
☎ 93 302 03 89
Metro Liceu
Open Mon.-Fri. 10am-2pm, 4.30-8pm, Sat. 5-8pm.

The oldest toy shop in the city; four generations of the Foyé family have kept the children of Barcelona happy over the years. There are metal toys for collectors and model horses in papier mâché (€72), musical boxes (€84), steam engines and fancy dress.

Drap
C. del Pi, 14 (C3)
☎ 93 318 14 87
Metro Liceu
Open Mon.-Sat. 9.30am-1.30pm, 4.30-8.30pm.

Few little girls will be able to resist these delightful doll's houses. Palaces, chalets and two-storey Victorian houses cost €240-2,400. Don't forget that once your dream house has been chosen, its walls have to be papered, fire-places have to be installed, curtains hung and finally it has to be furnished. Quite an expensive business!

Rosès
Avinguda del Portal de l'Angel, 15 (C2)
☎ 93 302 03 34
Metro Catalunya
Open Mon.-Fri. 9.45am-1.30pm, 4.30-8pm, Sat. 10.15am-2pm.

In a street where an angel is supposed to have once appeared, it isn't surprising to find a shop selling *figuras para belenes* (crib figures). The traditional cribs of Murcia and Olot (€36) always include a fertility symbol, the *caganer*, as described on p. 14.

Kiddy's Class

Via Augusta, 45 (C1)
☎ 93 237 96 12
Metro Diagonal
**Open Mon.-Sat. 10am-
8.30pm.**

A great choice of clothes at
unbeatable prices. Good value
sportswear with a hint of the
traditional and a touch of the
classroom. Shirts around €16,
T-shirts €9 and dresses €24.

Sardina Submarina

**C. del Cardenal Casañas,
7 (C3)**
☎ 93 317 11 79
**Open Mon.-Sat. 10am-2pm,
5-8.30pm**

This colourful shop behind the
Ramblas mainly specialises in
wooden toys – scooters, cookery
utensils and tea sets, puppets and
Danish mobiles, as well as board
games and lamps for all ages.

Oilily

C. del Tenor Viñas, 1 (B1)
☎ 93 201 84 79
Ferrocarril Muntaner
**Open Mon.-Sat. 10.15am-
2pm, 4.30-8.15pm.**

A riot of colour and pretty prints
will add a cheerful note to your
children's wardrobes, with
attractive little floral skirts,
checked lumberjack shirts, Sioux-
Indian-style sweaters, and

exclusive bikinis and swimwear.
The prices, however can be a little
on the high side.

Imaginarium

**Marina Village, 11 or
Rambla de Catalunya, 31 or
Maremagnum L40 (C1/2)**
☎ 93 487 67 54
**Open Mon.-Sat. 10am-
8.30pm.**

A colourful and brightly-lit setting
for open-air games – trampolines,
slides, swings and inflatable
swimming pools. And if you can't
imagine where you'd put it all,
you can fall back on the smaller
toys such as skittles, rocking
horses, spinning-tops, and drums.

Menkes

**Gran Via de les Corts
Catalanes, 642 (A/D2)**
☎ 93 318 86 47
Metro Passeig de Gràcia
**Open Mon.-Sat. 10am-
1.30pm, 5-8.30pm.**

Founded in 1950, Menkes is
the place to go for fancy dress
costumes, such as Sleeping Beauty,

El Ingenio

C. d'En Rauric, 6,
☎ 93 317 71 38.
Metro Liceu
**Open Mon.-Sat. 10am-
1.30pm, 4.15-8pm.**

A shop with a carnival
atmosphere. Since 1838,
the Cardona family have
been making masks and
cap-grossos, the giants' heads
that parade through the streets
of Barcelona and Sitges.
You can see a workshop at the
back of the shop where the
unfinished papier-mâché
heads have something very
bizarre and surreal about
them. Even Dali was fascinated
by this highly unusual place.

a toreador or a flamenco dancer –
with or without false eyelashes
(€66 to €90). It's an incredible
Aladdin's Cave, where children can
find just the outfit they want to
really make an impression at a
fancy dress party back home.

DEPARTMENT STORES AND SHOPPING ARCADES

Shops are usually open until around 7.30 or 8pm during the week and 6pm is a particularly busy time as people shop after work. However, don't forget that a few stores close for *siesta* after lunch (usually between 2 and 4.30pm), so don't expect all the shops to be open then. The newest stores and arcades, Maremagnum and Illa, have striking window displays, a source of great pride to the people of Barcelona.

like a vast Art Deco ocean liner. It's the city's biggest store and stocks a wide range of goods. However, be warned, prices are rather high and the ladies' fashion department is a little on the staid side. Still, if you can't find anything you like, you can always enjoy the view from the restaurant.

El Corte Inglés

Plaça de Catalunya, 14 (C2)
☎ **93 306 38 00**
Metro Catalunya
Avinguda Diagonal, 617 (C/D1)
☎ **93 419 28 28**
Metro Maria Cristina
Open Mon.-Sat. 10am-10pm.

This famous department store stands in the Plaça de Catalunya

Maremagnum

Moll d'Espanya (C3)
☎ **93 225 81 00**
Metro Drassanes
Open Mon.-Sun. 11am-11pm.

The most recent addition to the city's shore area and the pride of the people of Barcelona. This vast shopping centre has become an obligatory part of the Sunday stroll, with its mixture of cafés, restaurants, bars and shops. Maremagnum caters for all tastes, from the high-tech and kitsch to the eco-friendly and green. It's a bold construction of glass panels and wooden walkways.

Bulevard Rosa

Passeig de Gràcia, 55(C1/2)
☎ **93 215 83 31**
Metro Plaça de Gràcia.
Avinguda Diagonal, 474 (C/D1)
☎ **93 215 83 31**
Metro Diagonal
Open Mon.-Sat. 10.30am-8.30pm.

Hoping to find strength in numbers, the first shopping centres flourished in Barcelona, as in London, in the 1970s. There

and the Caprabo supermarket which sells food. It's not all that exotic for the visitor, but it's extremely practical for the locals due to its strategic location and large underground car park.

El Triangle

Carrer de Pelai, 39
☎ 93 318 01 08
Metro Universitat
Open Mon.-Sat. 10am-9.30pm (winter), 10am-10pm (summer).

The inauguration of this huge megastore, located right in the heart of the city, put an end to the derogatory nickname by which the area had become known – the 'block of shame'. It sells books, clothes and CDs, late into the evening and you'll find a good selection of international labels, including Habitat, Dockers, Camper and Agatha.

NO NEED TO WORRY ABOUT THE DEMISE OF THE LOCAL SHOP!

Like all cities, Barcelona suffers from the 'shopping centre' syndrome, yet Spaniards have never been in favour of mass marketing. They still prefer their traditional markets, and the city has no less than forty-one covered markets. The community spirit and various commercial groups combine to produce a network of resistance across the city and small retailers courageously fend off attacks from the big boys.

are over a hundred shops at these Boulevard Rosa locations. The fashion, shoe, jewellery and perfume boutiques and stores, along with cafés and bars make them favourite meeting places on Friday nights for teenagers and young professionals. The selection of shops tends to be fairly trendy and includes Marcel's, the 'in' place to have a haircut in Barcelona at the moment (a cut costs around €30 at the Avinguda Diagonal branch).

L'Illà

Avinguda Diagonal, 557 (C/D1)
☎ 93 444 00 00
Metro Maria Cristina
Open Mon.-Sat. 10am-9.30pm.

Located in the business district, on the Avinguda Diagonal, the three floors of this new shopping centre cater for the needs of the local office workers. You'll find many of the same shops that are in Maremagnum (see entry on left) are also to be found here, as well as Marks & Spencer

SPORTS GOODS AND GADGETS

The people of Barcelona take part in aquatic and mountain sports with equal enthusiasm. They're fanatical about football and balconies are decked with flags in the Barça colours during the football season. If you are particularly interested in sports goods and gadgets you will find plenty of choice here. In fact Barcelona had a very wide choice long before the Olympic Games came to town in 1992.

La Botiga del Barça

Maremagnum, L27
Moll d'Espanya (C3)
☎ 93 225 80 45
Metro Barceloneta
Open Mon.-Sun. 11am-10pm.

For ardent supporters of the local football team, you'll find football shirts, shorts, flags, caps, ash-trays and key rings in the Barça colours (red and blue). You can also visit the Camp Nou Stadium and museum (see p. 18) for that total Barcelona football experience.

Jonas

Carrer de Salvador Espriu,
L56-57 (D3)
☎ 93 225 15 68
Metro Ciutadella-Vila Olímpica
Open Mon.-Sun. 10am-10.30pm, Sat. 10am-11pm.

A red-chrome Harley Davidson in the entrance sets the tone and you know this is a shop for real enthusiasts. Jonas specialises in extreme sports and you can get your snowboarding and surfing gear here, made of either fleece or light nylon –

so, choose waves or moguls according to your mood.

Quera

C. de Petritxol, 2 (C2/3)
☎ 93 318 07 43
Metro Liceu
Open Mon.-Fri. 9.30am-1.30pm, 4.30-8pm, Sat. 10am-1.30pm, 5-8pm.

Leaf your way through a vast array of old maps and dusty tomes in this bookshop to discover interesting routes for your trekking expedition in the Pyrenees, or elsewhere. Familiarise

yourself with rock climbing, potholing, or more gentle pursuits – the adventure starts here.

Dos i Una

C. de Rosselló, 275
☎& 📠 93 217 70 32
Open Mon.-Sat. 10.30am-2pm, 4.30-8.30pm.

Behind an unprepossessing exterior lies an Ali Baba's cave in which you'll find small humorous gifts, souvenirs and gadgets. Just for your info, they are responsible for producing the famous BAR-CEL-ONA (Bar-sky-waves) T-shirt designed by Mariscal.

GADGETS

Items d'Ho

C. de Mallorca, 251 (A2)
☎ 93 488 32 37
Open Mon.-Sat. 10am-8.30pm
Passeig de Gràcia, 55
Bd Rosa (C1/2)
☎ 93 216 09 41
Open Mon.-Fri. 10am-8.30pm, Sat. 10am-3pm, 4-8.30pm.

This shop specialises in gifts for men. From key rings and luggage to fashionable glasses cases and chromium-plated watches, everything has been carefully designed to please your 'hombre'.

Natura

Maremagnum,
Moll d'Espanya (C3)
☎ 93 225 80 49
Metro Barceloneta
Open Mon-Sun. 11am-11pm
Consell de Cent, 304 (D2)
☎ 93 488 19 72
Open Mon.-Sat. 10am-8.30pm.

For fans of environmentally-friendly design, there are wood and rattan lamps, Mexican mobiles (€2.94), candle

holders, bird cages, Afghan hats and

T-shirts defending the rights of the whale – a little touch of Greenpeace – all wrapped up in recycled paper.

Dom

Passeig de Gràcia, 76 (C1/2)
☎ 93 487 11 81
Metro Passeig de Gràcia
Carrer Avinyó, 7
☎ 93 342 55 91
Open Mon.-Sat. 10.30am-8.30pm.

Wacky and unusual designs such as bags made from fun fur fabrics and brightly coloured nylon and pens that look like plastic flowers.

D Barcelona

Av. Diagonal, 367 (C/D1)
☎ 93 216 03 46
Metro Passeig de Gràcia
Open Mon.-Sat.10.30am-2pm, 4.30-9pm.
Maremagnum,
local 39 (C3)
☎ 93 225 80 86
Open Mon.-Sat.
11am-11pm.

The *Raiders of the Lost Ark* must have got their gear here. If you fancy going on a safari, camel expedition, jeep rally, or just like the 'Out of Africa' look, come along to the Colonel's and he'll supply you with everything you need. From the penknife to the survival kit, by way of the portable solar stove, you won't be short of anything next time you leave. *Bon viatge!*

An unusual shop packed with kitsch, practical, funny or zany gadgets, including sheepskin photo frames, fluorescent shower curtains and genuine leatherette sofas. Definitely just for fun.

DECORATION, TABLEWARE AND DESIGN

Barcelona is reputed for being at the forefront of innovative contemporary design, so capitalise on your weekend by acquiring a designer piece for your home. If you have very eclectic tastes, you won't be disappointed by what's on offer – colonial, country, high-tech, kitsch, utility, unusual or surrealist – as many styles as there are shops.

Punto Luz

C. de Pau Claris, 146 (C1/2)
☎ 93 216 03 93
Metro Passeig de Gràcia
Open Mon.-Fri. 9.30am-1.30pm, 4.30-8pm, Sat. 10am-1.30pm, 5-8pm.

No need to be kept in the dark, you'll find a sophisticated selection of lighting that will appeal to even the most demanding tastes. Say goodbye to those dreary old lampshades and dull colours. There are also lights and shades for the garden. Everything is bang up-to-the minute and fashionable.

Molsa

Plaça San Josep Oriol, 1 (C3)
☎ 93 302 31 03
Metro Liceu
Open Mon.-Sat. 10am-8pm.

At the foot of the Del Pi church steeple, Molsa has an authentic range of Spanish craft objects on display. – traditional ceramics from Galicia and Valencia, glassware from Majorca, blue-and-white checked window boxes, reproductions of 18th-century Catalan tableware, sundials, and colourful *azulejos*.

Beardsley

C. de Petritxol, 12 (C2/3)
☎ 93 301 05 76
Metro Liceu
Open Mon.-Sat. 10am-2pm, 4.30-8pm.

A shop window with an air of home-sweet-home about it, in this small lively street. Beardsley sells pot-pourri, dried flowers, petit-point embroidery, needlework, white Girona porcelain, bathroom accessories and, in the basement, a colourful range of cardboard storage boxes (€120-24), in flowery and checked designs and personalised writing paper (€3.58).

Cromía

C. d'Alfons XII, 7 (C1)
☎ 93 202 30 21
Open every day 10am-2pm, 4.30-8pm, closed Sun. & during August

You'll find everything ever made by the architect Oscar Tusquets in this shop. Admire the silk and cotton collection by Victoria Roqué and the jewellery made with precious stones by Luisa Delvalle as well as paper jewellery by Ana Hagopian.

a shady square in the Raval district, where two young designers happily produce a blend of craft and design. Hand-woven silk and cotton tinted with vegetable dyes are printed with exclusive, personalised designs. They're said to have 'good vibrations', so go ahead and treat yourself.

Juan Soriano Raura

Mayor de Gràcia, 53
(off map)
☎ 93 217 23 75
Open Mon.-Sat. 9am-2pm,
4.30-8pm.

When you leave the Passeig de Gràcia, make for this cut-price hardware shop. Dating from the 1890s, it's an Aladdin's Cave full of amazing bric-a-brac. Every item comes with detailed instructions for use and you're bound to find something you like amid the jumble that includes paella dishes, ramekins for *crema catalana* and *porronés*, which you drink from without letting the bottle touch your lips. A real curiosity shop.

Coses de Casa

Plaça San Josep Oriol, 5 (C3)
☎ 93 302 73 28
Metro Liceu
Open Mon.-Sat. 9am-2pm,
4.30-8pm.

If you have a strong liking for Catalan design, then this is the

place for you. In these antiquated surroundings you'll find a unique selection of Catalan fabrics, including the distinctive *llengos de Mallorca* in striking reds, blues and greens, with some promising materials in sunshine shades of golden yellow and coral pink.

Entre Telas

Plaça Vicenç Martorell, 1 (C2)
☎ 93 317 76 14
Open Mon.-Sat. 10am-2pm,
5-8pm.

A textile workshop that has taken up lodgings under the arcades of

Caixa de Fang

C. de Freneria, 1 (C3)
☎ 93 315 17 04
Metro Jaume I
Open Mon.-Sat. 10am-2pm,
4-8pm.

Behind the cathedral, gourmets will find all the utensils they need to concoct tasty Catalan dishes – salamander irons (€3.76), ramekins for *crema catalana*,

porronés, for drinking without letting your lips touch the bottle, olive-and-sand-coloured terracotta cooking pots, glazed ceramics and boxwood and olive-wood spoons (€0.75-1.95).

Servicio Estaciòn

C. d'Aragó, 270-272 (B/D2)
☎ 93 216 02 12
Metro Passeig de Gràcia
Open Mon.-Fri. 9.30am-2pm, 4.15-8pm, Sat. 9.45am-2pm, 4.30-8.15pm.

A gigantic hardware shop, where you'll find waxed cloth and plastic and Formica kitchen tiles. If you're looking for paella dishes (see p. 11), also try Juan Soriano Raura (see p. 99).

Taller de Lenceria

C. de Rosselló, 271 (C/D1)
☎ 93 451 39 52
Metro Diagonal
Open Mon.-Sat. 10am-2pm, 4.30-8pm.

Elegant table and bed linen made to measure in cotton, linen and lace, as well as a large selection of cotton piqué nightdresses and pyjamas on which you can have your initials embroidered.

Sit Down

C. de Mallorca, 331 (A2)
☎ 93 207 75 32
Metro Verdaguer
Open Mon.-Sat. 10am-1.30pm, 4.30-8pm.

You'll be spoilt for choice between re-issues of natural cane chairs by Oscar Tusquets and other designs

by Joseph Hoffmann, Philippe Starck and Jose Luis Luscà, making good use of colour and fabric and all reasonably priced (from €108).

Tierra Extraña

C. de Rosselló, 226 (C/D1)
☎ 93 487 95 88
Open Mon.-Sat. 10.30am-8.30pm.

As the name suggests, we're on foreign soil here, with Indonesian and colonial Indian furniture, parchment wall-lamps (€78), small raffia bedside lamps, palm basket work and craft objects displayed on low rattan tables that will make you believe you're in tropical climes.

Pilma

Av. Diagonal, 403 (C/D1)
☎ 93 416 13 99
Metro Diagonal
Open Mon.-Sat. 10am-2pm, 4.30-8.30pm.

Modern lifestyle in a contemporary transparent steel and glass setting. On the ground floor you'll find kitchen and bathroom accessories, on the first floor there's a passageway leading to a loggia full of light, colourful

THE VERY LATEST...

ASPECTOS
C. del Rec, 28 (D3)
☎ 93 319 52 85
Metro Jaume I
Open Mon.-Fri. 4.30-8pm,
Sat. 10.30am-2pm.

Interior designer Camilla Hamm's new gallery features up-and-coming young designers whose work is produced in limited editions. Come here to see some unusual pieces presented in elegant, sophisticated surroundings and find something just right for your home.

furniture. From pure wool tartan plaid fabrics to futuristic baskets, by way of the Noguchi paper lantern, Pilma clearly has plenty to offer.

Arkitektura
Via Augusta, 185 (off map)
☎ 93 362 47 20
🖷 93 241 17 85
Open Mon.-Fri. 9.30am-2pm, 4-7.30pm,
Sat. 10am-2pm, closed Sun.

This new space is dedicated to contemporary design for the home and office. In the large showroom you'll find a careful selection of the best of today's design. Arkitektura's mission is to marry avant-garde design with aesthetic appeal and a high degree of functionality. You'll find examples of furniture by all the latest designers – Alias, Armani, Depadova, Tecno and Azucena.

Zeta
C. d'Avinyò, 22 (C3)
☎ 93 412 51 86
Open Mon. afternoon-Sat. 11am-2pm, 5-9pm.

Kitsch is back and you can find it at Zeta's. Or, if you prefer, there's also a wide range of 'Peace and Love' and other 1970s-style items. Futons, artificial flowers, leopardskin lampshades, subdued lighting – that little bit of fun and of course bags of atmosphere. Friendly and amusing, not to be missed.

NOT FORGETTING...

Your visit would not be complete without seeing some of the design classics of yesterday and today. Try the BD boutique (Mallorca, 291) and Vinçon and Tinçon, sister shops found in Pg. de Gràcia, 96 and C. de Rosselló, 246, respectively (☎ 93 215 60 50, open Mon.-Sat. 10am-2pm, 4.30-8.30pm) where you'll find a huge range of original and modern objects for the home. Also try their website: www.vincon.com.

ANTIQUE DEALERS, SECONDHAND SHOPS AND FLEA MARKETS

From the bric-a-brac of an antique dealer to the open-air secondhand stalls in the Plaça del Pi, you'll discover the pleasures of bargain-hunting in the sun. You may not find the bargain of the century, but don't let that stop you bringing back something to remind you of Barcelona and the warm Mediterranean when you get back home.

Every Thursday from 9am-8pm (except in August), secondhand stalls set up shop in the cathedral square. Search hard and you may find some pretty *azulejos*, old ceramics, a doll with porcelain eyes, or carved whale teeth. Bric-a-brac with soul.

Mercat Sant Antoni
C. del Comte d'Urgell, 1 (B2)
☎ 93 423 42 87
Metro Sant Antoni
Clothes: open Mon., Wed., Fri. and Sat. 9am-7pm; Books: open Sun. 9am-2pm.

In an iron and glass hall dating from 1872, Sant Antoni's market is

Els Encants
Plaça de las Glòries (off map)
☎ 93 246 30 30
Metro Glòries
Open Mon., Wed., Fri. and Sat. 9am-5.30pm in winter, 9am-6pm (or 7pm) in summer.

The name 'Encant' comes from *cantar* (singing), as merchants here used to sing out the prices. Els Encants is a cross between a scrap metal yard and a jumble sale. There are bicycle wheels, books, old sofas, buttons, lamps – you name it, someone at Els

Encants will be selling it. A real flea market in the sun, but you'll need to get up early for the best finds.

El Bulevard dels Antiquaris
Passeig de Gràcia, 55 (C1/2)
☎ 93 215 44 99
Metro Passeig de Gràcia
Open Mon.-Sat. 9.30am-8.30pm.

In an elegant shopping centre in the Passeig, art lovers and collectors will find a clutch of good quality antique shops. It's a chance to take a quick look at a wide selection of quality items.

Mercat Gotic
Avinguda Catedral, 6 (C3)
☎ 93 291 61 18
Metro Liceu.

a bargain-hunter's paradise, where ladies who lunch happily rub shoulders with high-spirited teens, looking for clothes and accessories from eras before they were born. Every Sunday from 10am to 2pm, secondhand clothes change hands, and old editions of Tintin in Catalan, faded posters, colour prints and film magazines all vie for the favours of keen collectors. In one corner, they swap the latest characters from Japanese role playing games. There's something to suit all tastes here.

La Inmaculada Concepcion

C. de Rosselló, 271 (C/D1)
☎ 93 217 78 90
Metro Diagonal
Open Mon.-Sat. 10am-2pm, 4.30-8pm.

One of the pioneers of recycled furniture – *Modernista*, industrial and American-style office furniture – and also the designer of lamps with parchment lampshades.

Josep Pascual i Armengou

C. dels Banys Nous, 14 (C3)
☎ 93 301 53 65
Open Mon.-Sat. lunchtime 11am-1.30pm, 5-8pm.

The Banys Nous and Paja streets (Metro Liceu), in the heart of the old town, are crammed with interesting shops. Enter the maze and wander around to your heart's content. At Josep Pascual i Armengou you'll find early Catalan furniture, chests and *azulejo* tiles.

Gotham

C. de Cervantes, 7 (C3)
☎ 93 412 46 47
Open Mon.-Sat. 10.30am-2pm, 5-8.30pm.

A shop decorated in acid colours and translucent

URBANA

C. de Seneca, 13 (C1)
☎ 93 237 36 44
Metro Diagonal
Open Mon.-Fri. 10am-2pm, 4.30-8pm
No credit cards.

Right at the top of the *passeig*, in an extraordinary setting, you'll find relics salvaged from Spanish town houses (fireplaces from €1,500, plus bathroom accessories), old cinema seats, Chirico-style shop dummies, old shop signs and decorations. At Carrer de Còrsega, 258 you'll find Urbana, a shop specialising in old fireplaces.

plastic, selling furniture from the 1950s to 1970s to brighten up your world. Better than a course of vitamins and sure to banish the blues.

Erika Niedermaier

C. de la Palla, 11 (C3)
☎ 93 412 79 24
Open Mon.-Fri. 10.15am-1.30pm, 4.15-8pm, Sat. 11am-1.30pm.

Located in the narrow streets of medieval Barcelona, this shop sells delicate 17th-century ceramics, apothecary jars and a wide range of wrought-iron objects.

Maria José Royo

C. dels Banys Nous, 22 (C3)
Tienda, 1
☎ 93 302 35 20
Open Mon.-Fri.10am-1.30pm, 4.30-8pm, Sat. 11am-1.30pm.

Maria Jose Royo specialises in religious art, with a fine collection of gilded wood, sculptures and Baroque liturgical objects.

Rosa Cortés Interiors

C. de Pau Claris, 183
☎ 93 215 31 45
Open Mon.-Sat. 10am-1.30pm, 5-8pm.

This is the place to come if you like antique rustic furniture. It's like stepping into the countryside with its regional artisan pieces in Catalan wrought iron and Majorcan blown glass.

HOBBIES AND COLLECTIONS

You don't need to be particularly wealthy to be a collector, as long as you don't decide to collect Fabergé eggs that is, and some people do collect the strangest things. However, whatever your particular interest there's nothing quite like the pleasure of adding a foreign piece to your collection whilst on your travels.

A. Monge
C. dels Boters, 2 (C2)
☎ 93 317 94 35
Metro Liceu
Open Mon.-Sat. 9am-1.30pm, 4-8pm.

Philatelist or not, Monge is worth a visit for the *Modernista* shop front alone. Since 1904, Senor Monge has prided himself on his knowledge of coins and stamps. His collections include 1st and 2nd-century coins, and the more affordable sets of stamps of the Olympic Games (500 ptas).

Palau
C. de Pelai, 34 (C2)
☎ 93 317 36 78
Metro Catalunya
Open Mon.-Sat. 10am-1.30pm, 4.30-8.30pm.

A firm founded in 1935 selling the Scalextric, Meccano and Fleischmann brands. Everything is on a small scale here except the cashier and the prices. Expect to pay between €156 and €409 for an electric train. Have a look at the dozens of miniature electric lights – they're just like the real thing.

Megapuzzles
C. del Bruc, 68 (C2)
☎ 93 488 00 58
Metro Girona
Open Mon.-Sat. 10am-2pm, 4.30-8.30pm

If you're a puzzle fanatic, you really must make a visit to this store. It's dedicated to the passion for puzzles and sells nothing else. You'll find all sorts of examples, large and small, 3-D and in fluorescent colours. You'll also find the service is very personal.

Norma Comics
Passeig de Sant Joan, 7 (D2)
☎ 93 244 84 20
Metro Arc de Triomf
Open Mon.-Sat. 10.30am-2pm, 5-8.30pm.

Comic book collectors will find this store a good source for first editions, while fans of role-playing games, war games and *Star Wars* aficionados can stock up on cards, dice and accessories. If none of these spark any interest in you, you can always take a look at the Japanese printing machines which are also for sale.

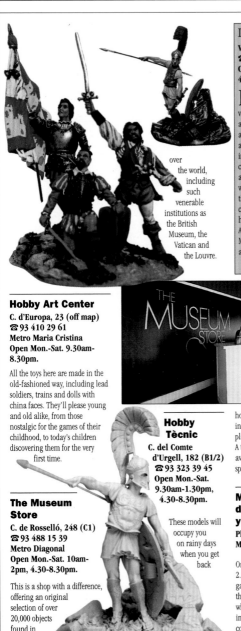

over the world, including such venerable institutions as the British Museum, the Vatican and the Louvre.

Hobby Art Center

C. d'Europa, 23 (off map)
☎ 93 410 29 61
Metro Maria Cristina
Open Mon.-Sat. 9.30am-8.30pm.

All the toys here are made in the old-fashioned way, including lead soldiers, trains and dolls with china faces. They'll please young and old alike, from those nostalgic for the games of their childhood, to today's children discovering them for the very first time.

The Museum Store

C. de Rosselló, 248 (C1)
☎ 93 488 15 39
Metro Diagonal
Open Mon.-Sat. 10am-2pm, 4.30-8.30pm.

This is a shop with a difference, offering an original selection of over 20,000 objects found in museum shops from all

Hobby Tècnic

C. del Comte d'Urgell, 182 (B1/2)
☎ 93 323 39 45
Open Mon.-Sat. 9.30am-1.30pm, 4.30-8.30pm.

These models will occupy you on rainy days when you get back home. Hobby Tecnic sells top international brands of model planes, boats and trains. A technical service is also available and there are even spare parts for sale.

Mercado de Numismatica y Filatelia

Plaça Reial (C3)
Metro Liceu.

On Sunday mornings (9am-2.30pm) coin and stamp collectors gather beneath the arcades of the Plaça Reial. Regardless of whether you have a particular interest in coin and stamp collecting, this is a very colourful market and a good place for a spot of people watching.

THE ART MARKET AND ART GALLERIES

The most important art galleries are situated in Carrer del Consell de Cent (between C. de Pau Claris and C. de Balmes), while newly fashionable areas, such as the Raval or Born, are witnessing the opening of new galleries spearheading the avant-garde. We suggest a few places, both legendary and visionary, to whet your appetite.

Sala Parès
C. de Petritxol, 5 (C2/3)
☎ 93 318 70 08
Metro Liceu
Open Mon.-Sat. 10.30am-2pm, 4.30-8.30pm, Sun. 11.30am-2pm.

The oldest art gallery in the city (1840), where the work of the great turn-of-the-century Catalan painters, such as Rusiñol, Casas, Nonell and Picasso, was exhibited. Each Sunday morning after attending mass, people would visit this avant-garde institution to discuss art, politics and religion. In 1928, Dali honoured it with his presence. A visit to this legendary place is essential for art lovers.

Galeria Maragall
Rambla de Catalunya, 116 (C1/2)
☎ 93 218 29 60
Open Mon.-Fri. 10am-1.30pm, 4.30-8.30pm, Sat. 10.30am-2pm, 5.30-8.30pm.

This gallery exhibits work by Catalan artists, in particular Tàpies and Miró from the older generation of artists and the more recent Castro and Enrick. It's also a good place if you are interested in lithographs. They have a very good collection and the prices aren't out of the question, starting at around €21.

Metronom
C. de la Fusina, 9 (D3)
☎ 93 268 42 98
Metro Jaume I
Open Tue.-Sat. 10am-2pm, 4.30-8.30pm.

This is the gallery of the famous collector Rafael Tous, which flourishes in the shadow of the Born market. It also houses a contemporary art foundation which is one of the keystones of cultural life in Barcelona.

Editiones T

C. del Consell de Cent, 282 (D2)
☎ 93 487 64 02
Metro Passeig de Gràcia
Open Tue.-Fri. 10am-2pm, 4-8pm, Sat 11am-2pm, 5-8.30pm.

Inaugurated in September 1994 by the son of Antoni Tàpies (see p. 29), this gallery specialises in original graphic works, books illustrated by artists such as Arroyo, Campano, Chullida, Le Witt and, of course, Tàpies.

Dels Ángels

C. dels Ángels, 16 (C2)
☎ 93 412 54 54
Metro Catalunya
Open Tue.-Sat. noon-2pm, 5-8.30pm.

Galleries flourish in the restored area of the Raval, thanks to the Museum of Contemporary Art, which helps young experimental artists to become established. A drawing by Santi Moix, for example, costs around €270, while paintings range from €901-3,125. A great place to spot new trends..

Ras

C. del Doctor Dou, 10 (C2)
☎ 93 412 71 99
Email: ras@oike.com
Metro Catalunya
Open Tue.-Sat. 1-9pm.

Ras is an interesting contemporary art gallery which hosts exhibitions and conferences on architecture, design and photography. The library is also very innovative and up-to-the-minute.

Cultural Centre of the Caixa-Palau Macaya Foundation

Passeig de Sant Joan, 108 (D1/2)
☎ 93 476 86 00
Open Tue.-Sat. 11am-8pm, Sun. 11am-3pm.

La Caixa is the fifth-largest non-profit making cultural institution in the world, hence its dynamism (see inset). Located in this remarkable *Modernista* palace, designed by Puig i Cadafalch, it has exhibition rooms, concert halls, reading rooms, sound archives, a video library, bookshop and bar.

La Caixa, not just a savings bank

Since 1990, La Caixa (pronounce the Catalan 'x' like the English 'sh') has become the second most powerful banking body in Spain. Omnipresent in the Arts and Sciences, it has revived the turn-of-the-century tradition of patronage. Its five-pointed blue star logo designed by Miró, hovers over the whole city, a symbol of the economic and cultural power of Catalonia.

CRAFT AND ECOLOGY

In Barcelona, as in many of the big cities of the world, people are hankering to return to a simpler way of life and are concerned with conserving the resources of the planet. In keeping with this you can now buy *organicas*, shirts made from Peruvian cotton, and *tortillas paisanas*, made of wheat. If you are into a 'green' lifestyle, you can pursue it in Barcelona just as well as in London or New York.

Hôma
C. del Rec, 20 (D3)
☎ 93 315 27 55
Metro Jaume I
Open Tue.-Fri. 5-9pm,
Sat. 11am-2pm, 5-9pm.

A former coffee warehouse in the Ribera has been converted into a very pleasant exhibition hall, with bedside lamps and exclusive eco-friendly wall lights in a primitive style, made of natural materials – raffia, wood and bamboo. The furniture by Ruben Vidal will add a 'recycled' touch to your home.

Indian
Passatge de Mercader, 16
(off map)
☎ 93 487 37 03
Metro Verdaguer
Open Mon.-Sat. 10.30am-2pm, 5-8.30pm.

Faience, delicate *azulejo* patterns created in the time-honoured way, embroidery, handmade carpets, traditional fabrics, Indian rice measures and colonial furniture. Those who appreciate a blend of cultures should come to Indian.

Arunachala
C. de Jovellanos, 1 (C2)
☎ 93 317 80 23
Metro Catalunya
Open Mon.-Fri. 9.30am-2pm, 4.30-8.30pm, Sat. 10.30am-2pm, 5-8pm.

This bookshop, a short walk from the Plaça de Catalunya specialises in the mysteries of the occult sciences, from Zen Buddhism to reincarnation and the New Age. There is a heady smell of incense on the air, which may encourage you to have your palm read and find out about your love life.

Dauer
C. dels Tallers, 48 bis (C2)
☎ 93 318 22 41
Metro Catalunya
Open Mon.-Fri. 10am-1.30pm, 4.30-8.30pm, Sat. 10am-1.30pm, 5-8.30pm.

The walls of this shop are lined with aquariums, full of colourful fish. They specialise in piranhas, sea horses and other marine and freshwater creatures here. Pay a

visit if you're feeling a bit stressed by the bustle of the streets outside and see if watching fish will have the required calming effect. Its a bit tricky to take a fish home with you, but if you feel so inclined, they range in price between €1.20 and €120.

The Living Stone

C. de Petritxol, 4 (C2/3)
☎ 93 318 35 67
Metro Liceu
Open Mon.-Fri. 10.30am-1.30pm, 5-8.30pm, Sat. 10.30am-2pm, 4.30-8.30pm.

This warm, sun-filled shop sells a range of eco-friendly cosmetics perfumed with the scents of the Spanish countryside and the Orient. The fragrances of bergamot, musk, honey, jasmine and patchouli fill the colourful glass bottles.

Cereria Subirà

Baixada de la Llibreteria, 7 (C3)
☎ 93 315 26 06
Metro Jaume I
Open Mon.-Sat. 9am-1.30pm, 4-7.30pm (closed Sat. pm).

In 1909, one of the city's oldest firms of candlemakers moved into this building constructed in 1847. Gilded panelling, two classic statues and an elegant staircase give it a timeless feel. Salvador Dali often used to come here, drawn by the old-fashioned atmosphere. The owner of Cereria Subirá is understandably proud of his hand-finished, natural beeswax candles costing from €0.90-12.

Herbolari Antiga Casa Guarro

C. d'En Xuclà, 23 (C2)
☎ 93 301 14 44
Metro Catalunya
Open Mon.-Fri. 9am-2pm, 4-8pm, Sat. 9am-2pm, 5-8pm.

If conventional medicines no longer have the required effect on your ailments, you can rediscover some age-old herbal remedies here. Also visit the natural products fair In the Plaça de Saint Josep, the first Friday and Saturday of every month.

BOOKSHOPS AND OFFICE ACCESSORIES

Of all the countries in Europe, the Spanish read the least number of books per head. Yet Barcelona is traditionally associated with novels and art book publishing and the city has five monuments dedicated to books, which are given as gifts on Sant Jordi's Day (see p. 15). Perhaps this might get the people reading?

Estilografica

C. de Fontanella, 17 (C2)
☎ 93 318 64 95
Metro Catalunya
Open Mon.-Sat. 9am-1.30pm, 4-8pm.

Founded in 1938, this shop has a fine selection of pens, biros and pen holders, *unica en precios y calidad*, as well as a workshop for repairs. Despite email, letter writing lives on.

Papirum

Baixada de la Llibreteria, 2 (C3)
Metro Jaume I
Open Mon.-Fri. 10am-8.30pm, Sat. 10am-2pm, 5-8.30pm.

Llibreria del Raval

Carrer d'Elisabets, 6 (C2)
☎ 93 317 02 93
Metro Catalunya
Open Mon.-Fri. 10am-8.30pm, Sat. 10am-2.30pm, 5-8.30pm.

This bookshop is located in the sanctuary of a former chapel, behind the new Museum of Contemporary Art. It resembles a vast library on whose shelves you can find almost anything and everything from large format art books, comic strip books and novels to more esoteric works.

Continuarà

Via Laietana, 29 (C2/3)
☎ 93 310 43 52
Metro Jaume I
Open Mon.-Sat. 10.30am-3pm, 4-9pm.

Two floors that are home to every kind of comic strip book you can imagine. The first floor is devoted to the more modern heroes, while the one below is devoted to the old favourites such as Zorro, Spiderman and Superman, who, despite being eighty years old, are just as agile as ever.

A small shop lit by a porcelain lamp containing some fine paper craft items made locally – seals, hand-made paper, boxes and diaries all lined with iridescent marbled paper. These items are exclusive to Papirum and are absolutely unique in the city (from €3-42).

La Central

C. de Mallorca, 237 (C/D1)
☎ 93 487 50 18
Metro Passeig de Gràcia
Open Mon.-Sat. 10am-9pm
(closed Sun.).

Located in a lovely apartment in the city centre, this international bookshop is dedicated to those interested in the humanities. It has a welcoming and intimate atmosphere and is a perfect spot for immersing yourself in works of literature, history, sociology, anthropology, philosophy, cinema and art (in several languages).

Tarlatana

C. de la Comtessa de Sobradiel, 2 (C3)
☎ 93 310 36 25
Metro Jaume I
Open Mon.-Fri. 9.30am-7pm.

In the Barrio Gòtic, Jaume Salvado has perfected the art of bookbinding and framing in the traditional way. The workshop upstairs is worth looking round. Tarlatana also has a selection of pens, diaries, blotters and coloured paper.

Llibreria Rodes

Carrer dels Banys Nous, 8 (C3)
☎ 93 318 13 89
Open Mon.-Fri. 10am-2pm,
4-8pm (call on Sat. before
visiting).

The tone is set as soon as you cross the threshold. From floor to ceiling, walls are lined with old works, out-of-print books and 18th-century engravings. A cat purrs happily in the corner and the atmosphere is calm and hushed. Entirely fitting for a bookshop set in the heart of the antiques district.

Llibreria Sant Jordi

C. de Ferran, 41 (C3)
☎ 93 301 18 41
Metro Jaume I
Open Mon.-Sat. 9.30am-2pm, 4.30-9pm.

Father and son have run this bookshop since 1880. The *Modernista* decor belongs to a bygone age. A warm welcome and

BOOK AND MAGAZINE PUBLISHING

Barcelona is really the centre of the publishing industry in Spain and the bulk of the printers, paper mills and publishers are to be found in and around the city. It's therefore no coincidence that Barcelona has given birth to a large number of publications, magazines and comic strip books, the latter being very much part of a tradition, if not a way of life in some non English-speaking European countries.

knowledgeable help guide you in your choice of works on art, architecture and design. Out of curiosity, take a look at the charming *calendari dels pagesos*, an astronomical and religious calendar, littered with nursery rhymes and sayings (€1.20).

GASTRONOMY

However you style yourself, gourmet, Epicurean, bon viveur, or just plain foodie, there is a great deal of scope for trying out new flavours in Barcelona and lots of opportunities to take some of these regional specialities home with you. Here are a few specialist shops for you to try.

Colmado Quilez

Rambla de Catalunya, 63 (C1/2)
☎ 93 215 23 56
Open Mon.-Fri. 9am-2pm, 4.30-8.30pm (cl. Sat. pm).

A traditional grocer's that's offered a wide choice of high-quality local products for the past fifty years. Bottles and tins are piled from floor to ceiling in a chaotic, old-fashioned but charming way.

Fargas

Plaça Cucurulla, 2 (C2)
☎ 93 302 03 42
Metro Catalunya
Open Mon.-Sat. 9am-1.30pm, 4-8pm.

A stone's throw from the cathedral, the pretty shop front of this confectioner's promises old-fashioned delicacies. They're still made the traditional way, using a millstone to produce powdered drinking chocolate. Among the specialities of the shop are *bombons de tardor, catanis* – almond, caramel and chocolate sweets which cost around €32.50 per kg/2.2lbs.

Comme-Bio

Via Laietana, 28 (C2/3)
☎ 93 319 89 68
Open Mon.-Sun. 9am-11pm.

As you may gather from the name, the products on sale at Comme-Bio exude well-being and health. They sell camomile, marjoram, thyme, passion-flower, organic chocolate, wholemeal bread and beer. There is nothing special about the setting, but you can also try the organic products on the premises.

Caelum

Carrer de la Palla, 8 (C3)
☎ 93 302 69 93
Open every day 10am-2pm, 5-8.30pm (closed Mon. am and Sun. pm) Restaurant open Tue.-Sat. 5-8.30pm.

A new and highly unusual addition to the antique district. *Caelum* advertises 'monastery delights and temptations'. An old-fashioned shop which boasts medieval recipes, communion wine and rose-petal jam.

All these delicacies are prepared in secret within the confines of the monasteries. You can try out these particularly divine specialities in a cellar occupying a former 14th-century public baths and also admire bed linen embroidered by nuns.

Planelles-Donat

Portal de l'Angel, 25 (C2)
☎ 93 317 34 39
Metro Catalunya
Open Mon.-Sat. 10am-8pm.
Curcurulla, 9 (C2)
Open Mon.-Sat. 10am-2pm,
4-8pm, Sun. 10am-2.30pm.

Since 1870, five generations of the Donat family have sold all kinds of *turrónes* (see box top right) in slabs as well as by weight to passers-by in the street. Their windswept stall gets packed at Christmas time, when the sweet-toothed people of Barcelona come out to treat themselves. *Turrón* makes an ideal, typically Catalan present to take back home with you.

J. Mùrria

C. de Roger de Lluria,
85 (D1/2)
☎ 93 215 57 89
Metro Passeig de Gràcia
Open Mon.-Sat. 10am-2pm,
5-8.30pm.

A visit to J. Mùrria is not only a feast for your taste buds, but also for your eyes. The wonderful selection of goods is displayed in an exceptionally well-preserved *Modernista* setting. Haunches of Guijuelo ham, nuts, extra virgin olive oil, jams and preserves from Penedès – all very tasty treats for a highly-refined palate.

La Viniteca

C. dels Agullers, 7 (C3)
☎ 93 268 32 27
Metro Jaume I
Open Mon.-Sat. 8.30am-
2.30pm, 4.30-8.30pm.

La Viniteca overflows with a range of full-bodied red wines (Rioja €3), fruity dry white wines (Penedès €3.60), local sparkling wines (Cava Codorniu brut €6), rosés, spirits, etc.

La Colmena

Plaça de l'Angel, 12 (C2)
☎ 93 315 13 56
Metro Jaume I
Mon.-Sun. 9am-9pm.

One of the few cake shops in the city specialising in sweets and soft caramels flavoured with eucalyptus, pine, thyme, fennel and coffee (€9 per kg/2.2lbs). Since the start of the century, this sweet-shop has sold nougat with crème brûlée (*de biema*), *panellets* in marzipan on

All Saints' Day, and treats to sweet-toothed people of all ages.

Nightlife Practicalities

Barcelona is inseparable from its bars and nightlife. Even the designer Mariscal reflected on this when he coined the Catalan play on words, 'Bar-cel-ona' (Bar = bar, cel = sky, and ona = wave). All across the city, bars and clubs come alive on a nightly basis. From cocktail lounges to jazz bars, from post-modern decor to disused hangars, you can listen and dance to every conceivable beat. Be prepared to be intoxicated by it all and party to the early hours.

WHERE AND WHEN?

Barcelona nightlife is constantly changing. Trendy places are quickly replaced by

new names, and cafes and bars succeed each other at an alarming rate. The people of Barcelona love going out, all age groups, all night and all year round. It's very difficult to recommend one district more than another because the hot spots vary according to the season. As you might expect, Thursday, Friday and Saturday nights are most popular. In summer, *carpas* (marquees) are erected in the port or stadiums, or even in

the city heights. Always spectacular, they have the

GETTING AROUND

Use taxis to get from place to place – they're affordable and available in vast numbers. The city is generally safe, except for the Barrio Chino (Chinatown), an area notorious for drugs and prostitution. Take a taxi if you go there after dark.

best bars of the season, and are definitely not to be missed.

HOW MUCH?

It's quite usual to only have to pay for your drinks, which makes it possible to move from place to place without seriously damaging your budget. If you have to pay to get into a club the price usually varies between €6-12, but the first drink is often free, or the person accompanying you may get in free. Cinema tickets are cheap (around €4.20 whereas theatre tickets are around €12).

SOME DOS AND DON'TS

Don't set off too early – most bars are dead before 11pm. It's also wise not to turn up at some of the clubs until 2am, otherwise you're likely to be the only person there! If the partying goes on until dawn, there'll always be a bar to serve you *chocolate con churros* or a baker's to cut up a crispy *pa de coca* to keep you going. By then, you'll have discovered that Barcelona rarely sleeps. The life of the hard-working, hard-playing Catalan can be yours, provided you can keep up with it.

HOW TO MAKE RESERVATIONS

If you want to make a last-minute booking for a concert or show, your hotel porter will help you, but you'll need to have an idea of what you want to see or you may end up saddled with his choice.

You can get information from *la Guia del Ocio*, and the *El Pais* and *la Vanguardia* newspapers, which will give you the prices and times of performances and the telephone numbers for bookings. For some shows, a 50% reduction is available three hours before the start of the performance. Enquire at the Tourist Information Office in the Plaça de Catalunya. Concerts at the Palau de la Musica are often very popular and seats need to be booked well in advance. As for the Liceu opera house, it has just been rebuilt after burning down for the third time in 1994.

THE BARCELONA LOOK

The discos and night clubs have no specific dress code, so you can wear what you like and if you're really partial to wigs and silk stockings, no-one will take offence. Barcelona is much less straight-laced and conventional than Madrid, so don't take too many smart clothes along for the evenings – concerts are really the only opportunities to dress up a little. As for restaurants, the atmosphere everywhere is very relaxed.

Tapas bars and late snacks

L'Arquer

Gran Via de les Corts Catalanes, 454 (B2)
☎ 93 423 99 08
Metro Rocafort
Open Tue.-Sun. 7pm-3am.

Tapas, copas y flechas, or how to pass an evening playing at Robin Hood! Four Olympic archery ranges (€7.20 for half an hour) allow you to demonstrate your great skill, while nonchalantly sipping on a 'magic-potion' cocktail.

La Bolsa

C. de Tuset, 17 (C1)
☎ 93 202 26 35
Metro Diagonal
Open Mon.-Fri. 8.30pm-3am, Sat. & Sun. 6pm-3am.

This bar has an innovative pricing system. Set up to work like the stockmarket, drinks are quoted like commodities and prices, displayed on screens, fluctuate according to the amounts consumed. An attractive brick and wood-panelled setting to watch your whisky on the rise!

Zig Zag

C. de Plató, 13 (off map)
☎ 93 201 62 07
Open every day 10pm-3am.

A classic bar that's been a favourite with the young people of Barcelona for twenty-one years. *Zig Zag*'s regulars opt for this trendy place that plays mainly jazz, funk and hip hop. Estrella and Ingrid will offer you a margarita or a pina colada, so why not sip on a cocktail, sit back and relax?

Schilling

C. de Ferran, 23 (C3)
☎ 93 317 67 87
Open every day 10am-2am.

Not far from the cathedral and fairly new, this is currently the 'in' place. Once an old knife factory, it has been turned into a very popular café. Exposed stonework, subdued lighting and bistrot tables make a very cosy setting for a cosmopolitan and gay clientèle. Try to get here around 8pm.

Replay Café

Passeig de Gràcia, 60 (C1/2)
☎ 93 467 72 24
Restaurant open every day 1-4pm, 8.30pm-2am (closed Sun. evening), *tapas* bar open all day.

Step into the hallway of this *Modernista* building and you'll be dazzled by the luxury of the decor. This is the place to come for some refreshment when you're out shopping. It's a combination of shop and restaurant that you'll want to visit more out of curiosity than for the cuisine.

The Quiet Man

C. del Marqués de Barbera, 11 (C3)
☎ 93 412 12 19
Open every day 6pm-2.30am.

Feeling nostalgic for an old Irish pub? Even in Barcelona you'll be able to drink a pint of foaming Guinness or a pure malt whisky in an Irish setting, with Celtic music at the weekend.

La Vinya del Senyor

Plaça Santa Maria, 5 (D1)
☎ 93 310 33 79
Open Tue.-Sun. noon-1am.

Situated on a charming square, this bar has one of the most pleasant terraces in the city. Enjoy local wines at candlelit tables, seated under the vines that give the bar its name. A delightful spot.

Casa Fernandez

C. de Santaló, 46 (off map)
☎ 93 201 93 08
Metro Diagonal
Open every day 1pm-1.30am.

If you suddenly feel hungry in the course of your night-time wanderings, try Casa Fernandez for a quick bite, where you can sample a selection of cold sausages and hams or a creamy *tortilla* washed down with the local Penedès wine. You'll soon be ready for more!

Hans Bar

C. de Muntaner, 473 (C1/2)
☎ 93 211 17 13
Closed Mon. evening, Sun. and Holy Week.
Metro Universitat.

This restaurant becomes a bar at 1am and is a regular spot for a local, rather up-market clientèle. In Barcelona people tend to gather in venues in their own district, and these can vary greatly from one area to another.

El Salon

C. de l'Hostal d'En Sol, 6 (C3)
☎ 93 315 21 59
Metro Jaume I
Open Mon.-Sat. 1pm-3am.

El Salon is a friendly bar opening onto a little street behind the post office. Its the cheerful blend of odd chairs and tables, Baroque chandeliers, exposed stonework and a comfortable old sofa that make this an ideal setting for homemade pastries or warming a bowl of vegetable soup until as late as 3am.

El Japones

Passatge de la Concepció, 2 (C1)
☎ 93 487 25 92
Lunchtime: Mon.-Fri. 1.30-4pm, Sat. & Sun. 1.30-5pm.
Evenings: Mon.-Sun. 8.30pm-midnight, Fri. & Sat. 8.30pm-1am.

Enjoy delicious Japanese food in a trendy Zen environment seated at large shared tables with wooden benches. The kitchen opens onto the dining area so you can watch the chefs at work.

Escribà

Litoral Mar, 42 (off map)
☎ 93 221 07 29
Open Tue.-Fri. 1-4.30pm, Sat. noon-6pm, Sun. noon-11pm.

Since 1906 Escribà has specialised in home-made sweets and pastries – praline-flavoured chocolates and bitter chocolate cream slices – washed down with a cup of Ethiopian coffee. In this *chiringuito* (seaside restaurant) there are plenty of mouth-watering dishes for you to try.

Un coche menys

C. de Esparteria, 3 (D3)
☎ 93 268 21 05
Sat.-Sun. setting off at 10am, returning at 12.30pm (€ 12), Tue. and Sat. setting off at 8.30pm, returning at midnight (€ 30).

How to explore the city, stay fit and help protect the environment. On Tuesday and Saturday evenings dozens of people set off on bikes in pursuit of a guide, criss-crossing the city in all directions. Aperitif and dinner are included and afterwards there's dancing. It's a good, easy way to get to know the Catalans and a few unusual places. All you need is a passport and the right sportswear.

Late bars and all-night bars

Velòdrom

C. de Muntaner, 213 (C1/2)
☎ 93 430 51 98
Metro Hospital Clinic
Open Mon.-Sat. 6am-2am.

From night to morning this 1940s bar attracts a cosmopolitan clientele. Time has blackened the walls and patinated the furniture, but the back room is a haven for billiard fans all night long. Bags of atmosphere.

Nick Havanna

C. de Rosselló, 208 (C/D1)
☎ 93 215 65 91
Metro Diagonal
Open Sun.-Thu. 11pm-4am,
Fri.-Sat. until 5am.

Nick likes to boast that this is 'the ultimate bar'. In any case, it has live music on Thursdays, salsa and samba classes on Tuesdays, a Catalan book vending machine, if you feel like trying to read, and a pendulum describing the movements of the earth, all in a designer decor. If you like trendy places, this is for you.

Le Marsella

C. de Sant Pau, 65 (C3)
☎ 93 442 73 63
Metro Liceu
Open Mon.-Thu. 9pm-2.30am,
Fri.-Sun. 6pm-2.30am.

Located in the Raval district, Indiana Jones would feel quite at home in this bar. Its original decor, old mirrors, bistrot chairs and marble tables create quite a nostalgic atmosphere. At the weekends a fortune teller will read the cards for you.

London Bar

C. Nou de la Rambla, 34
☎ 93 318 52 61
Metro Liceu
Open Tue.-Sun. 7pm-4am.

The Raval district (beware of pickpockets) has fortunately preserved this bar, which opened in 1910 and where Picasso used to come on his nightly wanderings. The decor with the patina of time, tobacco smoke and jazz rhythms are reminders of the former Bohemian lifestyle. On some evenings, a trapeze artist whirls through the air in memory of the artists of the Barcelonés circus, which was destroyed during the Civil War.

Snooker

C. de Roger de Llúria, 42 (D1/2)
☎ 93 317 97 60
Metro Urquinaona
Open every day 6pm-3am.

A splendid red and gold decor, with subdued alabaster lights, Riart armchairs dotted around and, as you might imagine, a number of snooker players. A stylish setting for a mojito or Hawaiian cocktail.

Zsa-Zsa

C. de Rosselló, 156 (C/D1)
☎ 93 453 85 66
Metro Diagonal
Open Mon.-Sat. 9pm-3am.

The kilim-covered walls are a blaze of colour, and together with the studied lighting and pale birchwood partitions, the decor adds a touch of magic to the place. You can sip a cocktail at the bar on a tall metal stool while listening to the salsa rhythms, which complete the atmosphere.

Dot

C. Nou de Sant Francesc, 7 (C3)
☎ 93 302 70 26.

Currently one of the best places, with a great DJ and film shows projected on the dance floor. A trendy place you shouldn't miss that's full to bursting every weekend. *Buenas copas y muchas risas* – good drinks and plenty of laughter!

Insolit

Maremagnum, L111 (C3)
☎ 93 225 81 78
Metro Barceloneta
Open Mon.-Sun. 1-11pm, nightclub until 5am.

With its futuristic decor, this cyber café is an internet bar for late nights on the web. Half an hour's connection to anywhere in the world costs €2.40.

Tres Torres

Via Augusta, 300 (off map)
☎ 93 205 16 08
Funicular Tres Torres
Open Mon.-Thu. 5pm-3am, Fri.-Sat. until 4am.

In summer, the terraces and garden of this splendid *Modernista* villa turn it into a magical place, with little tables and bamboo armchairs set out under the palm trees. The ideal place to sip a glass of punch in the moonlight.

Almirall

C. de Joaquin Costa, 33 (C2)
☎ 93 412 15 35
Metro Liceu
Open every day 8pm-2am.

Only a short walk from the Museum of Contemporary Art, this bar in the Raval has kept its original, pleasant *Modernista* setting. Local regulars congregate round the little bistrot tables or sit on the battered sofas.

La Fira

C. de Provença, 171 (B/D1)
Metro Hospital Clinic
Open Mon.-Thu. 1pm-midnight, Fri.-Sun. 1pm-5am.

One of our favourite places. If you're nostalgic for the atmosphere of *La Strada*, you'll love the La Fira bar. An enthusiast brought the bric-a-brac of a disused fun-fair here piece by piece – distorting mirrors, arcade machines, a fortune teller, trapezes and roundabouts, all with a tale to tell. For those who love poetry in motion.

Mirablau

**Avinguda de Tibidabo
(off map)
☎ 93 418 58 79
At the foot of the funicular.
Open every day 11-5am.**

This bar with its panoramic
view is a must to round off a
romantic evening. From 2am
onwards, couples gather on the
terrace and gaze at the lights of
the city twinkling in the distance.
A timeless classic.

Partycular

**Avinguda de Tibidabo, 61
(off map)
☎ 93 211 62 61
Open Wed.-Sun.
7pm-midnight.**

A *torre* and villa with romantic
seaside decor high in the city
hills. Order a cava under the
palm trees before taking a tour
of the property.

El Born

**Passeig del Born, 79(D3)
☎ 93 319 57 11
Metro Jaume I
Open every evening
8pm-12.30am.**

The Plaça del Born is *the* place
for anyone wanting to spend a
night on the town. A tour of the
bars is a must, with the El Born,
El Copetin and Miramelindo all
vying for the favours of those
intent on pleasure. You can dance,
sip cocktails and set the world to
rights until the wee small hours,
if you have the stamina.

Rosebud

**C. d'Adria Margarit, 27
(off map), Av. de Tibidabo
☎ 93 418 88 85
Open Mon.-Fri. 9pm-4am,
Sat.-Sun. 7pm-5.30am.**

Rosebud takes its name from the
last word uttered by the hero
of *Citizen Kane* and doesn't
refer to the bar's setting. It's an
ideal place to come on a mild
summer evening, nevertheless,
when the enormous glass dome
makes a pleasant setting.

Gimlet

C. del Rec, 24 (D3)
☎ **93 310 10 27**
Open Mon.-Sat. 8pm-3am.

In the 1970s Gimlet put new life into cocktails. The understated decor, with its glass cabinets and wooden bar pays discreet homage to New York cocktail bars of the 1930s. Connoisseurs know they serve the best dry Martinis in the city here.

Torres de Avila

Av. Marquès de Comillas (A2)
☎ **93 424 93 09**
Metro Espanya
Open Fri & Sat. 11pm-5am.

Some talented designers have converted the two towers of the entrance to the Pueblo Espanol. Bars, billiard rooms and terraces decorated with stars by Mariscal are arranged on several levels like a set of Russian dolls. The panoramic view from the rooftop terraces is a must in summer.

Palau Dalmases

C. de Montcada, 20 (D3)
☎ **93 310 06 73**
Open Tue.-Sat. 8pm-2am, Sun. 8-10pm.

A sumptuous Baroque setting in an aristocratic palace on the Montcada, a stone's throw from the Picasso Museum. Gleaming mirrors, the scent of musk, amber and iris, bowls of fresh fruit and garlands of flowers bathed in candlelight turn the weekly concert of Baroque music into a dream.

Cabarets, jazz, and shows

La Boite

Av. Diagonal, 477 (C/D1)
☎ **93 419 59 50**
Open every day 11pm-5.30am.

The best jazz cellar in the city, with a 1970s decor and knowledgeable audience, presents legendary artists such as Lou Benett, Dr Feelgood and jazz musicians from all over the world, as well as bands playing funk-jazz, hard-soul, reggae, blues, etc. After the concert, the fevered atmosphere of the disco takes over.

La Tierra

C. d'Aribau, 230 (C1/2)
☎ **93 414 27 78**
Open Thu.-Sat. 11pm-5am.

Smart and clean but beginning to show its age, this is one of Barcelona's more trendy places, with something for every musical taste. Take your pick from salsa, rumba, funk, acid-jazz, swing, country and blues.

Tarantos

Plaça Reial, 17 (C3)
☎ **93 318 30 67**
Shows Mon.-Sat. at 10pm
Entry charge €22.84.

Flamenco isn't popular with Catalans, but it you want to see this Andalusian dance during your stay then Los Tarantos are the unrivalled masters of the art. Their singing and guitar playing and the artistry of the dancers make a wonderful show.

Jamboree

Plaça Reial, 17 (C3)
☎ **93 301 75 64**
Open every day 9pm-5am.

Housed in the vaults of a former convent, this was the first jazz club opened in Spain, in 1959. It has long since swapped the cornet for the saxophone, and blues, Dixieland and New-Orleans jazz have made way for the pulsating rhythms of funk.

LA BODEGA BOHEMIA

C. de Lancaster, 2 (C3)
☎ **93 302 50 61**
Open every day 11pm-3am.

Donde nacen los artistas ('where stars are born') the sign outside boldly declares, but with Rosa from Granada vocalising, Valentin the Catalan dancer sketching a few steps and syrupy Juan José singing 'Lola Lolita' as he has for the past twenty-five years, there's not much chance of that! You'll have the place more or less to yourself, apart from two or three old dears in the audience. A touching performance for tender hearts and sensitive souls.

Salsitas

C. Nou de la Rambla, 22 (B/C3)
☎ 93 318 08 40
Metro Parallel
Open Tue.-Thu. 8pm-2.30am, Fri. & Sat. 8pm-4am, Sun. 8pm-2.30am.

An interesting and original venue, with a white decor, that serves Mediterranean cuisine. At midnight it's transformed into one of the trendiest clubs in the city, with house music played by a cool DJ. The atmosphere is pretty wild, so put yonour glad rags and dance the night away.

Nightclubs and discos

Universal

C. de Maria Cubí, 184 (B1)
☎ 93 201 35 96
Open Mon.-Sat. 10pm-4.30am.

Opened in 1985 this is still the trendiest place in Barcelona, but beware of the decibel level. This is a classic bar with designer decor. There are always queues to get in, but they are quite choosey about whom they will admit.

Otto Zutz

C. de Lincoln, 15 (off map)
☎ 93 238 07 22
Open Tue.-Sat. from midnight.

Situated in an old warehouse, this club has six bars and an enormous dance floor on three levels. They vet hopeful entrants at the door– you'll only get in if they like the look of you. An interesting mix, from football stars to artists and designers. They sometimes have bands playing live here.

Bikini

C. de Deu i Mata, 105 (B1)
☎ 93 322 00 05
Tue.-Sun. from 11.30pm.

Situated under the Illa centre, 1,200m^2/13,000sqft of floor space on two levels houses a concert hall, a dance floor and a calm lounge for quiet conversation. After falling into decline, this legendary Barcelona nightspot has risen from the ashes more vibrant than ever.

Up and Down

C. de Numancia, 179 (off map)
☎ 93 205 51 94
Tue.-Sat. from midnight.

The place to come if you're with your parents – upstairs for them and downstairs for you. It's how the Barcelona middle classes solve the generation gap. Everyone under the same roof but each to his own. Wear a tie and dine to music upstairs, or wear what you like and drink Coca-Cola downstairs.

Luz de Gas

C. de Muntaner, 246 (C1/2)
☎ 93 209 77 11
Open Fri. & Sat. until 6am, Sun. 10pm, opera concerts.

This former Belle Epoque theatre has been turned into an enormous dance and concert hall, with the upper gallery a pleasant place for a quiet chat or tasty *bocadillo* (Spanish-style sandwich). The clientele ranges from 7 to 77.

Mirabé

**C. de Manuel Arnús, 2
(off map, Tibidado)**
☎ 93 434 00 35
Open every day 7am-3am.

Have a drink in the romantic garden with its panoramic view over Barcelona. This music bar is located in the city heights and

is a trendy venue for well-heeled and glamorous regulars. It's quiet and intimate on the first floor, but if you fancy dancing the night away to your favourite tunes from the 1980s, head downstairs.

La Paloma

Carrer de Tigre, 27
☎ 93 301 68 97
Open Thu.-Sun. evenings.

A legendary dance hall with all the charm of yesteryear that's well worth a visit. Everything could be classed as of historical interest here, from the smooth crooners of the orchestra with their greying, slicked-back hair to the stucco ornamentation of the balconies.

Music

L'Auditori

C. de Lepant, 150 (off map)
☎ 93 247 93 00
www.auditori.com
Credit card ticket sales:
☎ 902 10 12 12

This building, designed by the architect Rafael Moneo, opened in 1999, and with its perfect acoustic, has become a reference point in the world of classical music, satisfying even the most demanding of music lovers. It has two concert rooms – not to be missed!

Palau de la Musica

C. de Sant Francesc
de Paula, 2 (C2)
☎ 93 295 72 00
Metro Urquinaona.

If you're a classical music lover, find out what's on the programme at this magnificent concert hall as soon as you arrive in the city. The splendid *Modernista* decor by Domenech i Montaner is also worthy of close attention (see p. 40, Ribera).

Places not to miss in the Barrio de Gràcia

We recommend a tour of one of the city's most popular districts, the Barrio de Gracia, which is little frequented by tourists. Spared by the rebuilding for the Olympics, it retains much of its original charm. A former suburb of little houses and gardens, it has preserved its character thanks to its squares, covered markets, cafés and the Lliure theatre. Leave the metro at Fontana station and follow our guide.

Sol Soler

Plaça del Sol, 13 (C1)
☎ 93 217 44 40
Open Mon. & Tue. 7pm-midnight, Wed.-Sun. noon-midnight.

On the Plaça del Sol, there are at least half a dozen bars occupying the terraces. To start the evening, you can try mouth-watering *tapas* – chicken wings in sweet and sour sauce, tabbouleh with fresh herbs, and vegetable and fish pâté. Bistrot tables, checkered tiles, and whirring fans set the scene for tasty food and local wines.

Virreina

Plaça Virreina, 1 (off map)
☎ 93 237 98 80
**Open every day 10am-
1.30am.**

There's a village atmosphere on the terrace, located on one of the prettiest squares in the area. Families enjoy it here at lunchtime, but it gets more lively in the evening, particularly before or after a film in the nearby Verdi cinema.

Tons

**C. dels Xiquets de Valls, 14
(off map)**
☎ 93 237 78 20
**Open Mon.-Sat. 10am-2pm,
5-8.30pm.**

This is an inspirational place for those interested in interior decoration. They sell lights, lampshades and doorknobs in original shapes and colours. If you want to try your hand at some decorative painting there are paints, brushes and stencils. They also have an interesting line of table linen.

Café del Sol

Plaça del Sol, 16 (C1)
☎ 93 415 56 63
**Open every day 1pm-
2.30am.**

Sit on the terrace of the bar and see what's going on in the square – old people gossiping and taking a walk in their slippers, children playing ball and young couples smooching happily on the benches.

Bodega Manolo

**C. de Torrent de les Flors,
101 (D1)**
☎ 93 284 43 77
**Open for lunch Tue.-Sat.,
dinner Thu.-Sat.**

A truly authentic, traditional *bodega*, where you sit at a neon-lit bar to drink the local wine, unless you happen to have brought along a bottle to fill from one of the barrels. If you have time, have a plate of grilled green asparagus, tuna carpaccio and grilled cuttlefish with mushrooms. With checked tablecloths and the locals all around you, it's a slice of Barcelona life to savour to the full.

LLIURE THEATRE

**C. del Montseny, 47
(off map)**
☎ 93 218 92 51
**Metro Fontana
Open every day except Mon.**

Since 1976, this former cooperative has been home to the prestigious 'Free Theatre', with performances strictly in Catalan. You can always get round the language barrier by opting to see a performance of contemporary dance instead of a play.

Sabor Cubano

C. de Francesco Giner, 32
☎ 93 217 35 41
Open every day 9pm-3am.

After a warm welcome, you'll feel as if you've just landed in the Caribbean. On Wednesday evenings a live orchestra invites you to step into the spotlight and dance to the salsa beat. All the flavour of Cuba right here in the Gràcia.

Fronda

C. de Verdi, 15
☎ 93 415 20 55
**Open every day exc. Tue. 8pm-
1am (to 3am at weekends).**

Close to the Verdi cinema, one of the few places to show films in the original language, Fronda takes care of its appearance, with a mahogany bar, subdued lighting, rattan armchairs and tables, a relaxed atmosphere and a jazz accompaniment.

Conversion tables for clothes shopping

Women's sizes

Shirts/dresses

U.K	U.S.A	EUROPE
8	6	36
10	8	38
12	10	40
14	12	42
16	14	44
18	16	46

Sweaters

U.K	U.S.A	EUROPE
8	6	44
10	8	46
12	10	48
14	12	50
16	14	52

Shoes

U.K	U.S.A	EUROPE
3	5	36
4	6	37
5	7	38
6	8	39
7	9	40
8	10	41

Men's sizes

Shirts

U.K	U.S.A	EUROPE
14	14	36
$14^{1}/_{2}$	$14^{1}/_{2}$	37
15	15	38
$15^{1}/_{2}$	$15^{1}/_{2}$	39
16	16	41
$16^{1}/_{2}$	$16^{1}/_{2}$	42
17	17	43
$17^{1}/_{2}$	$17^{1}/_{2}$	44
18	18	46

Suits

U.K	U.S.A	EUROPE
36	36	46
38	38	48
40	40	50
42	42	52
44	44	54
46	46	56

Shoes

U.K	U.S.A	EUROPE
6	8	39
7	9	40
8	10	41
9	10.5	42
10	11	43
11	12	44
12	13	45

More useful conversions

1 centimetre	0.39 inches	1 inch	2.54 centimetres
1 metre	1.09 yards	1 yard	0.91 metres
1 kilometre	0.62 miles	1 mile	1. 61 kilometres
1 litre	1.76 pints	1 pint	0.57 litres
1 gram	0.035 ounces	1 ounce	28.35 grams
1 kilogram	2.2 pounds	1 pound	0.45 kilograms

This guide was written by **Marie-Ange Demory**.
This edition was updated by Virginia Pulm, with the collaboration
of Aurélie Joiris and Élodie Louvet
Translated by **Christine Bainbridge**. Revision of English edition
Jane Moseley. Additional research and assistance: Georgina Hawkes,
Michael Summers and Christine Bell. Copy editor **Margaret Rocques**.
Series editor **Sofi Mogensen**.

We have done our best to ensure the accuracy of the information contained in this guide.
However, addresses, phone numbers, opening times etc. inevitably do change from time
to time, so if you find a discrepancy please do let us know. You can contact us at:
hachetteuk@orionbooks.co.uk or write to us at Hachette UK, address below.

Hachette UK guides provide independent advice. The authors and compilers do not accept any
remuneration for the inclusion of any addresses in these guides.

Please note that we cannot accept any responsibility for any loss, injury or inconvenience
sustained by anyone as a result of any information or advice contained in this guide.

Photo acknowledgements

Inside pages: **Laurent Parrault**: p. 2 (t.c.), 3 (c.c., b.l.), 10 (t.r., b.l.), 11, 12 (t.r., c.c., b.r.), 13 (c.l., b.r.), 14, 15, 16 (t.l., b.l.), 17 (t.l.), 18, 19, 20, 21 (t.l., b.), 22 (t.r., b.c.), 23 (b.l., b.r., c.r.), 24 (t.r.), 25 (b.c., c.l.), 28 (c.l., t.r. J.Miró © ADAGP, Paris 1997), 29 (t.r., c.l., b.c.), 30, 31, 37, 38, 39 (t.r.), 40 (b.r.), 41, 42 (b.l., b.c.), 43 (t.c., b.c.), 44 (b.l., c.r.), 45 (t.l., c.c.), 46 (t.r.), 47 (c.l., b.l.), 48 (b.l.), 49 (b.r., t.r.), 50, 51 (b.c.), 52 (t.r., t.l., b.r.), 53 (t.c., c.l., b.r.), 54 (c.r.), 55 (t.l., t.c., b.r.), 56, 57, 58, 59, 60, 61 (t.l., t.r.), 62 (c.c., b.l.), 63 (t.l., c.l., c.c., b.r.), 64, 65 (b.r.), 66, 67 (t.l. © J. Miró, ADAGP, Paris 1997, b.l.), 68 (b.ll., b.r.), 69 (c.l., b.c.), 76 (b.l.), 78 (c.c.), 79 (c.c., b.l., b.r.), 80 (c.l.), 81 (c.r.), 86 (t.r., c.r.), 87 (b.l.),88 (t.c., b.l.), 90, 91, 92 (t.r., b.r.), 93 (t.c., t.r., c.l.), 94 (t.r.), 95 (b.r., b.l.), 96, 97, 98 (t.r.), 100, 102 (t.c., b.r.), 103 (b.c.), 104 (t.r., b.r.), 106, 107 (b.c.), 108 (t.r., b.l.), 109 (t.l.), 111 (c.r.), 112 (t.r., c.l., b.l.), 113 (t.l., c.c., b.r.), 116 (t.l.), 117, 118 (t.l.), 119, 120 (c.l., b.l.), 121 (t.l., b.r.), 122, 123 (t., c.c.), 124. **Christian Sarramon**: p. 3 (b.l.), 10 (c.r.), 12 (c.l.), 13 (t.l., c.r.), 16 (t.r.), 17 (b.r.), 22 (b.c.), 23 (t.c.), 24 (b.l., b.r.), 25 (t.l.), 29 (b.r. © J. Miró, ADAGP, Paris 1997), 36, 39 (b.c., c.l.), 40 (c.l.), 42 (c.c.), 44 (c.l.), 45 (b.r.), 46 (b.l.), 47 (t.r.), 48 (c.c., b.r.), 49 (t.l., b.l.), 51 (t.c., c.r.), 52 (c.r.), 54 (b.l.), 55 (c.r., b.l.), 61 (c.l., c.r., b.r.), 62 (b.r.), 63 (t.r.), 65 (c.c., c.l., t.r.), 67 (t.r.), 68 (c.r.), 69 (t.r., b.r.), 78 (b.r.), 86 (b.r.), 87 (t.r.), 92 (b.l.), 93 (c.c., b.r.), 94 (c.l., b.c.), 98 (b.c.), 99 (c.c., b.r.), 102 (c.r., b.l.), 103 (t.r., c.l.), 104 (c.l.), 109 (b.l., b.r.), 113 (b.l.), 118 (b.), 120 (t.r.), 121 (b.l.). **Éric Guillot**: p.98 (c.l.), 108 (c.c.).
Hachette Livre: p. 28 (b.r. © succession Picasso, Paris 1997), 40 (t.r. © succession Picasso, Paris 1997), 42 (t.r. © ADAGP, Paris 1997. **C. Sarramon/Maison de Marie-Claire**: p. 16 (c.r.) **Arca de l'Avia**: p. 21 (c.r.) **Boutique BD**: p. 25 (c.r.) **Karin Wagner**: p. 26 (t.r.) **Ana Hagopian**: p. 26 (c.r.) **Chelo Sastre**: p. 26 (b.) **Ruth**: p. 27 (t.c.) **Nani Marquina**: p. 27 (c.l.) **Antonio Miró**: p. 27 (b.c.) **Clara Uslé**: p. 27 (b.r.) **Ici et La**: p. 43 (b.l.). **Moska**: p. 43 (c.r.) **Gran Teatre del Liceu © Antoni Bofill**: p. 47 (c.c.) **Fundació Caixa Catalunya © Pau Giralt-Miracle**: p. 51 (t.l.) **Tinçon**: p. 52 (b.l.). **Restaurant Tragaluz**: p. 53 (t.l.). **Hotel Arts Barcelona**: p. 72 (t.l.). **Hotel Condes de Barcelona**: p. 72 (c.r.). **Hotel Claris**: p. 72 (b.l.). **Hotel Metropol**: p. 73 (t.r.). **Hotel Gran Derby**: p. 74 (c.l.). **Hotel Montecarlo**: p. 74 (t.r.). **Hotel Rivoli Ramblas**: p. 74 (b.l.). **Hotel Romàntic**: p. 75. **Semproniana**: p. 76 (b.r.). **Reial Club Maritim**: p. 77 (t.r.). **Flash Flash © Leolpoldo Pomés**: p. 77 (c.l.). **La Balsa**: p. 78 (b.l.). **Agua © Jordi Sarrá Arau**: p. 79 (t.r.). **Taxidernista**: p. 80 (c.r.). **La Estrella Sitges**: p. 81 (b.r.). **Forum**: p. 86 (b.l.). **Groc**: p. 87 (t.l.). **Lydia Delgado © Ugo Camera**: p. 87 (b.r.). **Noténom**: p. 88 (b.r.). **Rafa Teja Atelier**: p. 89 (t.r.). **Hipótesi**: p. 89 (c.l.). **Cristina Castañer**: p. 89 (b.l.). **Rosa y Francesc**: p. 89 (b.r.). **Bulevard Rosa**: p. 94 (c.r.). **L'Illa**: p. 95 (t.l.). **Entre Telas**: p. 99 (t.l.). **Arkitectura**: p. 101 (t.l.). **Vinçon**: p. 101 (c.). **Rosa Cortés Interiors**: p. 103 (c.r.).**Hobby Art Center**: p. 105 (t.l., b.c.). **Museum Store**: p. 105 (c.r.). **Editiones T**: p. 107 (t.l.). **La Caixa**: p. 107 (c.r.). **Cereria Subirà**: p. 109 (c.r.). **Tarlatana**: p. 111 (b.). **La Central © Eva Bellapart**: p. 111 (t.l.). **Caelum**: p. 112 (t.r.). **Replay Café**: p. 116 (b.r.). **L'Auditori © Roger Velázquez**: p. 123 (b.l.).
Front cover: **Laurent Parrault**: t.l.; c.r.; c. J. Miró © ADAGP, Paris 1997; c.r.; b.l.; b.r. **J.M. Foujols, Stock Image**: t.c. (figure). **C. Bouvier, Stock image**: c.c. (figure). **C. Maeder, Pix**: b.c. (figures). **Christian Sarramon**: c.c.
Back cover: **Laurent Parrault**: t.r.; c.c. (lamp). **Christian Sarramon**: c.l.; b.c.

Illustrations Pascal Garnier   **Cartography** © Hachette Tourisme

Distributed in the United States of America by Sterling Publishing Co., Inc.
387 Park Avenue South, New York, NY 10016-8810

A CIP catalogue for this book is available from the British Library

ISBN 1 84202 170 2

Hachette UK, Cassell & Co., The Orion Publishing Group, Wellington House, 125 Strand,
London WC2R 0BB

Printed and bound in Italy by Milanostampa

If you're staying on and would like to try some new places, the following pages give you a wide choice of hotels, restaurants and bars, with addresses.

Although you can just turn up at a restaurant and have a meal (except in the most prestigious establishments), don't forget to book your hotel several days in advance (see p. 70). Enjoy your stay!

(see p. 70)

STAYING ON A LITTLE LONGER

Please note that prices given are a guide only and are subject to change.

Barcelona

Gran Hotel Catalonia★★★★
C. de Balmes, 142
☎ 93 415 90 90
🖷 93 415 22 09
Metro Diagonal.
This hotel in a strategic setting near the Diagonal and Passeig de Gràcia is one of the most traditional in the city. With many years' experience behind it, it will please those who like old-fashioned service. It also has a car park.

Calderon★★★★
Rambla de Catalunya, 26
☎ 93 301 00 00
🖷 93 317 31 57
Metro Passeig de Gràcia.
In a marvellous setting on the Rambla de Catalunya, a stone's throw from the city's most popular shops, the Calderon offers the practical comfort of designer rooms with parquet flooring. There are also 15 luxury suites.

Majestic★★★★
Pg de Gràcia, 68
☎ 93 488 17 17
🖷 93 488 18 80
www.hotelmajestic.es
Metro Passeig de Gràcia.
This hotel in the stately Passeig de Gràcia is one of the city's classics. Recently renovated inside, it still has a turn-of-the-century façade and its reputation has remained intact.

Ambassador★★★★
C. de Pintor Fortuny, 13
☎ 93 412 05 30
🖷 93 302 79 77
Metro Liceu.
A stone's throw from the Ramblas and the Boqueria market in a typical Barcelona street, this hotel offers charming views, impeccable service and a swimming pool.

Gran Hotel Barcino★★★★
C. de Jaume 1/6
☎ 93 302 20 12
🖷 93 301 42 42
Metro Jaume 1.

If you're looking for a medium-sized hotel (53 rooms) offering 4-star service in the Barrio Gotico, then this is the place to come. Ask for a quiet room away from the noise and bustle of the street.

Balmes★★★
C. de Mallorca, 216
☎ 93 451 19 14
🖷 93 451 00 49
Metro Passeig de Gràcia.
If you're staying in the city in the summer months, this hotel has the enormous advantage of having a swimming pool and small garden. Around a hundred modern rooms and a supervised car park make it a practical and convenient place to stay.

De l'Arc★★
La Rambla, 19
☎ 93 301 97 98
🖷 93 318 62 63
Metro Drassanes.
Near Plaça de Catalunya, this neat little hotel with 45 rooms is both pleasant and practical. Good value for money and not to be missed.

Messon Castilla★★
C. de Valdoncella, 5
☎ 93 318 21 82
🖷 93 412 40 20
Metro Catalunya.
In an alley in the Raval, a stone's throw from the Museum of Contemporary Art, this Spanish inn has made every effort to stay kitsch in a trendy district. 56 rooms with a rustic Castilian decor and a supervised car park.

Cortès★★
C. de Santa Anna, 24
☎ 93 317 91 12
🖷 93 302 78 70
Metro Catalunya.
This 45-room hotel offering a warm welcome and basic comfort is in the pedestrian area of Santa Anna. Quiet at night and lively in the daytime, it's ideal for exploring the city on foot.

Roma Reial★
Plaça Reial, 11
☎ 93 302 03 66
🖷 93 301 98 39
Metro Liceu.

An inexpensive hotel in an imposing setting. From the 52 rooms with a view of the square you can watch the comings and goings of life in the Barrio Gòtic night and day. The Quinze Nits restaurant is close by and just as affordable (see p. 79).

Comercio★
C. d'Escudellers, 15
☎ 93 318 74 20
🖷 93 301 98 39
Metro Liceu.
With the same owner as the Roma Reial, this inexpensive little hotel is impeccably clean and quiet. Well located in the old part of the city, it's perfect for people on a budget. The same is true of the La Fonda restaurant in the same street.

If you'd like to stay outside Barcelona, you'll find a choice of hotels in Sitges, Torrent, San Agaro and Aiguablava in the selection below. (The telephone code is the same for calling Barcelona: 00 34.)

Sitges

La Renaixença*
Isla de Cuba, 13
☎ 93 894 83 75
🖷 93 894 81 67.
If you want to spend your break in this idyllic little seaside resort (40km/25 miles from Barcelona), you can stay all year round at this Modernista villa with its elegant, old-fashioned decoration and a charming turn-of-the-century atmosphere. Not to be missed.

San Agaro

Hostal de la Gavina*****
Pl. de la Rosaleda
☎ 97 232 11 00
🖷 97 232 15 73.
One of the finest luxury hotels on the Costa Brava, with antique furniture and old masters adorning the walls. Peace and quiet in a luxury setting are the order of the day, with tennis, a swimming pool, a sauna and excellent cuisine. Uninterrupted view of the sea. An hour and a quarter from Barcelona.

Torrent

Mas de Torrent*****
Finca Mas del Rei
☎ 97 230 32 92
🖷 97 230 32 93.
There are 30 suites decorated with contemporary paintings in this 18th-century farmhouse. A swimming pool and tennis courts, with opportunities for horse riding and golf nearby, make a pleasant way to extend your weekend in Catalonia. 130km/80 miles north of Barcelona, near Bisbal.

Aiguablava

Aiguablava****
Platja de Fornells
17255 Begur
☎ 97 262 20 58.

Four successive generations have built the reputation of this hotel on the Costa Brava. Children's activities, volley-ball, a seawater swimming pool and direct access to the beach make it the ideal place for families. 150km/95 miles north of Barcelona, near Gerona.

Generally speaking, the prices shown are for a complete meal, not including drinks. Please note that some places only take cash and that the prices are a guide only.

Ribera

Salero
Carrer del Rec, 60
☎ 93 319 80 22
Open Mon.-Sat.
This former tuna-salting warehouse brings a breath of New York to the Santa María del Mar district. It naturally serves tuna tartare and Japanese-style dishes based on fresh vegetables. The set lunch is good value at €6.60.

Hofmann
C. d'Argenteria, 74-78
☎ 93 319 58 89
Closed Sat. and Sun.
Originally a cookery school , Hofmann is now one of the best restaurants in the city. Come here to sample new Mediterranean cuisine by Mey Hofmann, who concocts delicious gourmet dishes. Around €51.

Raval

Selenus
C. dels Angels, 8
☎ 93 302 26 80
Open Mon.-Sat., closed Sun. and Mon. evening.
Not far from the Museum of Contemporary Art and the ideal place to nourish body and soul after a morning spent studying abstract art. You can enjoy grilled salmon with fresh vegetables.

L'Eixample

La Vaquería
C. de Deu i Mata, 141
☎ 93 419 07 35
Open every day except Sat. and Sun. lunchtime.
For fans of the rustic-style, this former barn has been stylishly renovated with carefully chosen bric-a-brac. Milk churns and bales of hay make it feel like the set of a western film – appropriately enough since

Vaquería means cowshed. There's also a disco and a piano bar. The lunch menu features fish tartare and fresh market produce.

Gràcia

Botafumeiro
C. del Gran de Gràcia, 81
☎ 93 218 42 30
Open every day.
A Barcelona seafood institution, with lobsters, crabs, sea spiders, Galician percebes and sea bass. A very traditional decor but a very lively bar. Allow €48-60 each.

Taberna del Cura
C. del Gran de Gràcia, 83
☎ 93 218 17 99
Open every day.
A very rustic-style restaurant with exposed brickwork and hams, strings of garlic and onions hanging from the ceiling just for decoration. The menu itself specialises in meat, with Catalan sausages, shoulder and ribs of lamb that are grilled in front of you. À la carte meal costs around €21.

Café Salambo
Carrer de Torrijos, 51
☎ 93 218 69 66
Open every day.
A stone's throw from the Verdi, one of the few cinemas in the city to show films in the original language, this restaurant in the Gràcia (see p. 50) is very welcoming, with its subdued lighting, wooden seats and traditional-style stews. The owner tells endless stories about the district. Set lunch €8.40.

Mesopotamia
C. de Verdi, 65
☎ 93 237 15 63
Open Mon.-Sat.
Don't miss this trendy new restaurant serving Iraqi cuisine – dolma, curries, vegetables in season and meat kebabs served on designer plates Gourmet set meal €15.

Envalira
Plaça del Sol, 13
☎ 93 218 58 13
Open Tue.-Sat. for lunch and dinner, Sun. for lunch.

Don't overlook this local restaurant with its regulars and traditional dishes – arroz a la marinera (rice), grilled cuttlefish, monkfish with prawns and cockles. An ordinary setting, but good food and a warm welcome. Set meal at around €18.

The city heights

Can Cortada
Av. de l'Estatut de Catalunya
☎ 93 427 23 15
Open every day.
In summer, take advantage of the light breeze from the hills to sit on the terrace of this 11th-century farmhouse. The menu combines produce from the land and the sea, including chicken with prawns, Catalan-style cod with beans, and pig's trotters. Around €30. Come by taxi.

Vivanda
C. Major de Sarrià, 13
☎ 93 203 19 18
Open Tue.-Sat.
Ideal in summer when you can take advantage of the lovely, shady terrace. Often full to bursting, with the €7.81 set lunch attracting office workers from the area. Excellent value for money at lunchtime.

Barrio Gòtico

Culleretes
Carrer de Quintana, 5
☎ 93 317 30 22
Open Tue.-Sat and Sun. lunchtime.
This is the ideal place to celebrate a birthday, wedding anniversary or other special occasion. The waiters dressed in white jackets are happy to give advice on what to order – they have been serving torrades with garlic and tomatoes and graellades for years and so know what they are talking about. Set lunch from €12.60-24.

Juicy Jones
C. del Cardenal Casanas, 7
☎ 93 302 43 30
Open every day.
The vegetarian set meal at €7 varies every day. It's currently a good deal, so do make the most of it. The psychedelic decor and

two waitresses who look as if they're just back from Katmandu are charming. You can come in simply to have a soya or fresh fruit milkshake and, as a bonus, have your cards read in the back room. A stone's throw from the Ramblas and the Plaça del Pi.

Café de l'Académia
Carrer Lledo, 1
☎ 93 319 82 53
Open Mon.-Fri., for breakfast as well.
With its stone walls and exposed beams, subdued lighting and red glazed tiles, this is a very welcoming place. The menu is tempting, too, and you won't be able to resist the artichoke and parmesan soup, mushroom risotto and green asparagus salad (€21). Enjoy!

Ateneu Gastronomic
C. del Pas de l'Ensenyança, 2 bis
☎ 93 302 11 98
Open Mon.-Sat. lunchtime.
The regulars from the nearby Town Hall have made this their local. Colleagues who want to get to know one another gather round Mediterranean specialities, including dishes from Portugal, Aragon and Ampurda. It's a friendly, relaxing place, with a well-stocked cellar (enoteca) that loosens tongues and makes you want to stay on. Around €18.

BARS

Pas del Born
C. de Calders, 8
☎ 93 319 50 73
Open every night (exc. Sun.).
This bar in the trendy Born district (Ribera) is really more of a music-hall, with variety shows twice a month, flamenco singers and dancers every Friday, and, on Wednesdays and Saturdays, nonchalantly-swinging trapeze artists, who may invite you to dance.

Café Kafka
C. de la Fusina, 7
☎ 93 310 05 26
Open every night (exc. Sun.).
This newly-converted warehouse a stone's throw from the Born market is reminiscent of New York. You have to come late, as with all the Born bars. You can have dinner first at the nearby and equally trendy Salero (see previous pages).

Glaciar
Plaça Reial, 3
☎ 93 302 11 63
Open every day.
An ideal meeting-place for those who start the nightly round of the bars in the older districts of the city. A vast terrace with a cosmopolitan and bohemian atmosphere.

Pipa Club
Plaça Reial 3, principal
☎ 93 302 47 32
Open every night from 10pm.
A private club which is open to the public. It has a very British atmosphere with pipe-smokers in the sitting room, in keeping with the club's name. There are also occasional jazz and blues concerts.

DISCOS

Jazzmatazz
Passatge de Domingo, 3
Open Wed.-Sat. 10pm-4am.
All kinds of events take place here, including theatre and dance. This is a relatively new venue which provides live music most nights, including jazz, blues and funk.

Luna Mora
C. de la Marina, 19
☎ 93 221 61 61
Open Wed.-Sun. 10.30pm-5am in summer; Thu.-Sat. 11.30pm-5am in winter.
A recently-opened disco near the Arts Hotel in Port Olímpic. For the past two years, this has been one of the city's hottest nightspots, with disco music, 80s revival, and live broadcasts in a lunar-inspired decor.

Dietrich
C. de Consell de Cent, 255
☎ 93 451 77 07
Open 6pm-2.30am.
A colourful café, disco and gay bar frequented by a sometimes provocative clientèle.

BARS/CAFÉS

A SHORT WALK IN THE BARRIO GÒTICO

Start from *Santa Maria del Mar*, (D3, see p. 41) a delightful church at the bottom of the Carrer de Montcada in *La Ribera*. Continue up the Carrer de Montcada until you reach the beautiful medieval *Museu Picasso* (see p. 40) on the right-hand side. A little further up the street you will come to the junction with the Carrer de la Princesa, turn left here and continue across *Plaça de l'Angel.* You are now on the Carrer Jaume I (C3), from where you turn right onto the Carrer Freneria which will take you up to the cathedral (see p. 36). Pause here to admire the cathedral, or the *Seu*, as it is known. This is one of Spain's greatest Gothic buildings. Opposite you can see a frieze by Picasso portraying people dancing the *sardanas*, the traditional Catalan dance. This is the heart of the *Barrio Gòtico* in the old town.

Cross the large square in front of the cathedral, the *Plaça Nova*, and head for the *Palau Episcopal* on the square's western side, This is the former Bishop's Palace. You can't go inside, but can see the façade with its fine outer staircase. From the Bishop's Palace take the Carrer de la Palla until you reach the delightful *Plaça Sant Josep Oriol*, and stop for a drink at the *Bar del Pi* (see p. 81).

At the weekend you may find the square given over to an artist's market with street musicians and entertainers. If you don't fancy a drink at the bar here, try the adjacent *Plaça del Pi* where you can sip *horchata*, a typically Catalan drink made from barley. Take a look at the church of *Santa Maria del Pi* (see p. 38). Built in the 14th century, it was burned down in 1936, but restored in the 1960s. It is mainly gothic in style, but has a Romanesque door and some impressive stained glass windows inside.

From here continue along the Carrer de Cardenal Casanas which will take you to the Barrio's legendary street, *La Rambla* (C2). Turn right and you will see the covered market *La Boqueria* (see p. 47), a little further up on the left. This is a must for all food lovers. Even if you don't buy any of the cheeses, hams, spices, nuts or dried fruit on sale, it's a real pleasure to see local produce well displayed and to gain an idea of the kinds of food Catalans eat every day.

On leaving the market, turn right and walk back down *La Rambla* until you come to the *Gran Teatre del Liceu* (see p. 47) on the right. It has had a troubled past. First built in 1847, then rebuilt after a fire in 1861, it was regarded as the finest opera house in Spain. However, in 1893 it was bombed by an anarchist and destroyed again, killing twenty people at the same time. Finally, it was accidentally burned down once more in 1994. Since then it has been restored again, so keep your fingers crossed for its future in the new millennium.

Back on *La Rambla*, walk on a little further and turn right onto the Carrer Nou de La Rambla (C3). On the left-hand side you will see the *Palau Güell* (see p. 45), one of Gaudi's many buildings in the city. Don Eusebio Güell, Gaudi's most important patron, commissioned it in 1885. It is now a museum dedicated to Gaudi's and other *Modernista* architects' ideas. Most of Gaudi's buildings are still in private hands, so it is quite rare to be able to visit their interiors. You can remedy the situation therefore, by visiting this museum. The *Palau Güell* was the first modern building to be designated a world heritage site by UNESCO. When you leave the building, just glance across the street to no. 6. This is where Picasso's studio was located in 1902 and from where he began his Blue Period. Incidentally, Picasso did not like Gaudi's work at all.

Walk back up the street to join *La Rambla* once more. This time, cross the road and take the Carrer Colom, leading off *La Rambla* which takes you into *Plaça Reial* (C3, see p. 47). This elegant square in the Italianate style was constructed around 1850 according to plans by Frances Daniel Molina. It has iron street lamps by Gaudí and a fountain depicting the Three Graces at its centre. Rather down at heel and seedy at one time, the square was frequented by drug pushers, drunks and troublemakers, but was cleaned up in the 1980s. It still has its fair share of eccentrics and the odd dubious-looking character, but it is a great place from which to watch people and, on the terraces of one of its cafés or bars, to relax after your walk.

A SHORT WALK

NOTES